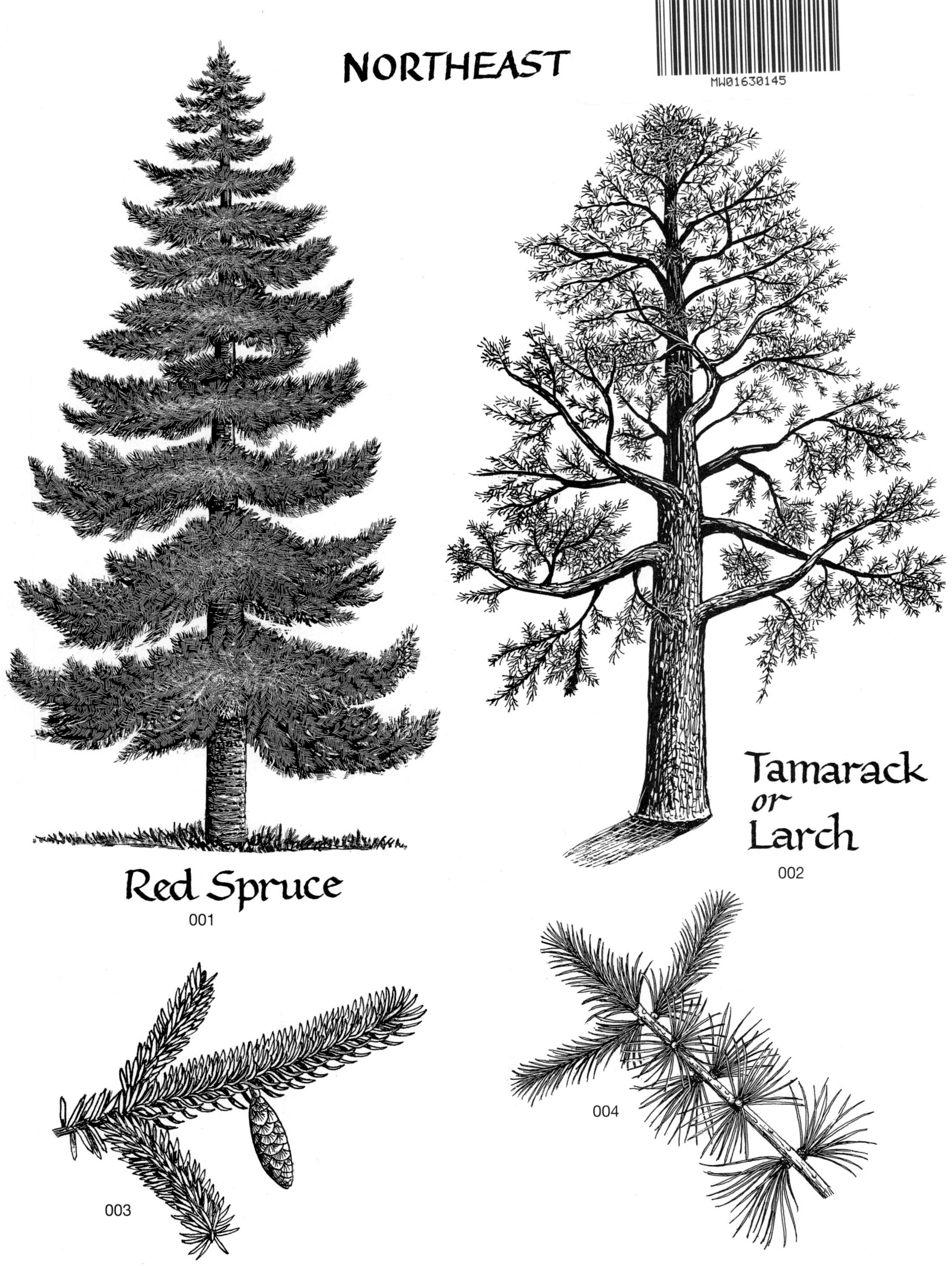

Red Spruce
001
Tamarack
or
Larch
002
003
004

SOUTHEASTERN PINES

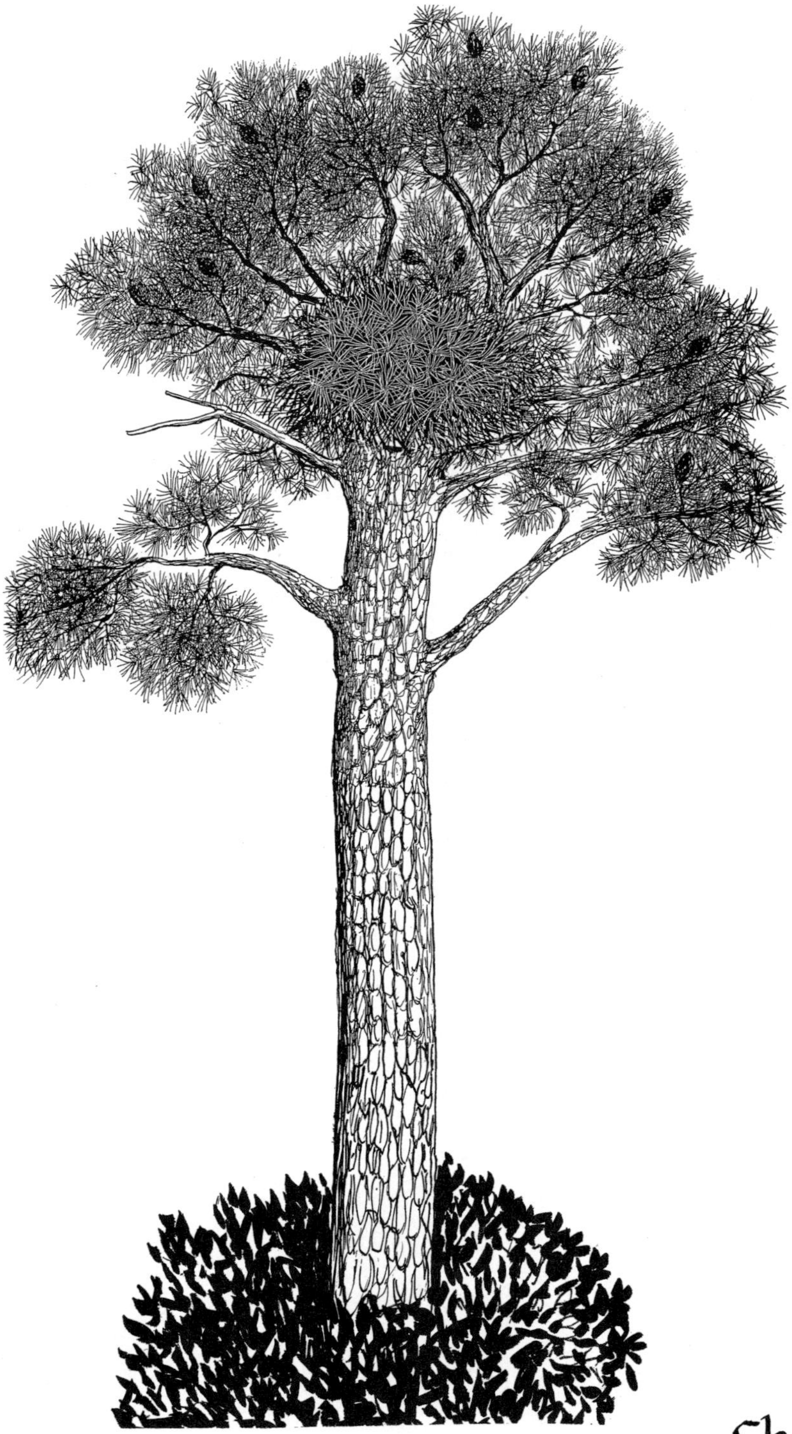

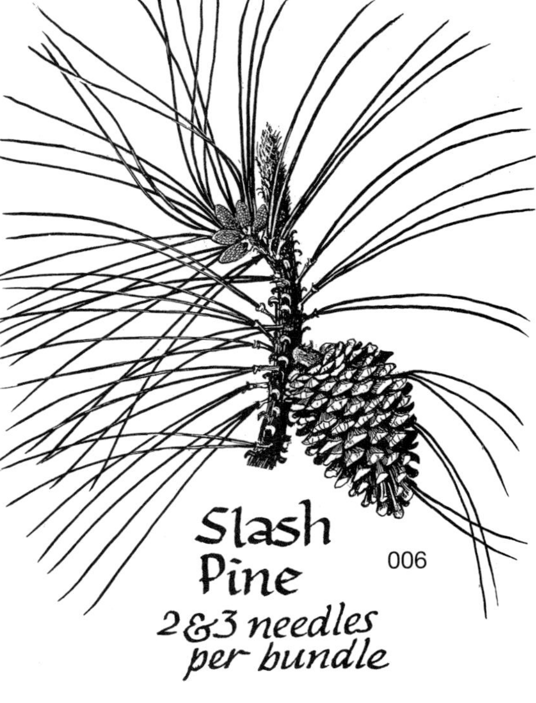

Slash
Pine
006
2 & 3 needles
per bundle

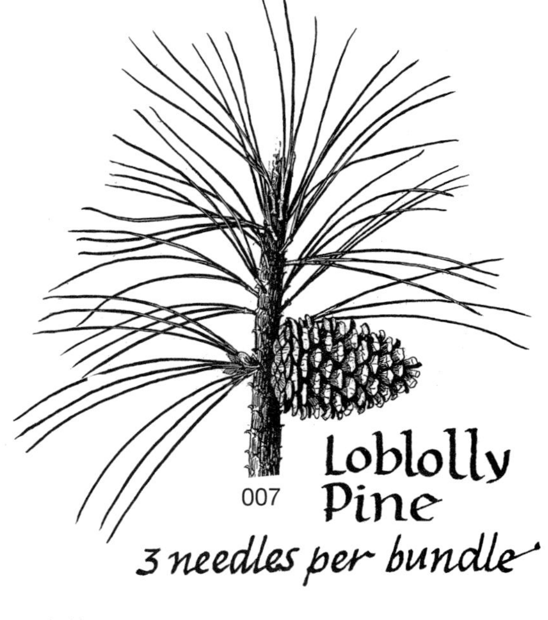

Loblolly
Pine
007
3 needles per bundle

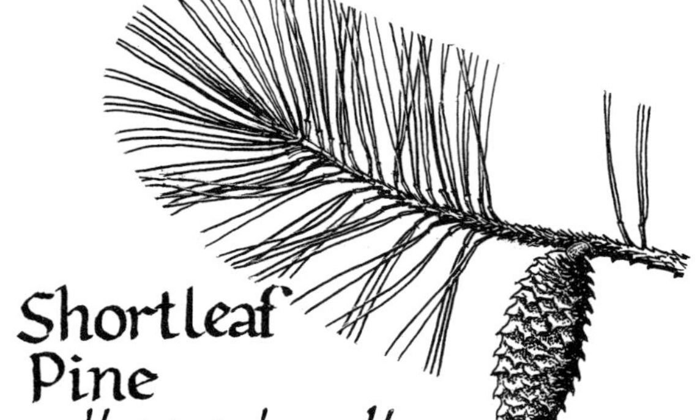

Shortleaf
Pine
2 & 3 needles per bundle
008

005

SOUTHEAST Longleaf Pine Forest

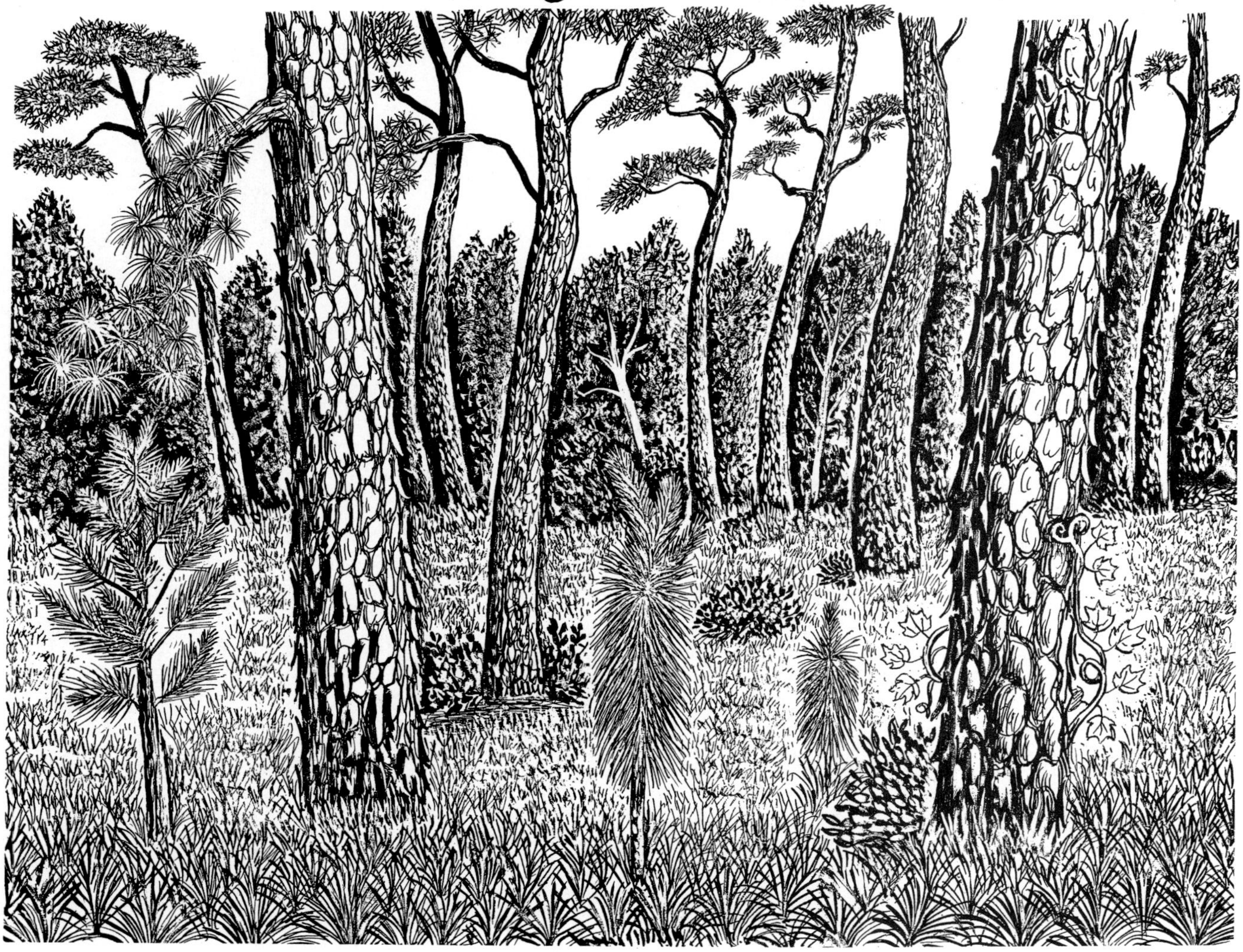

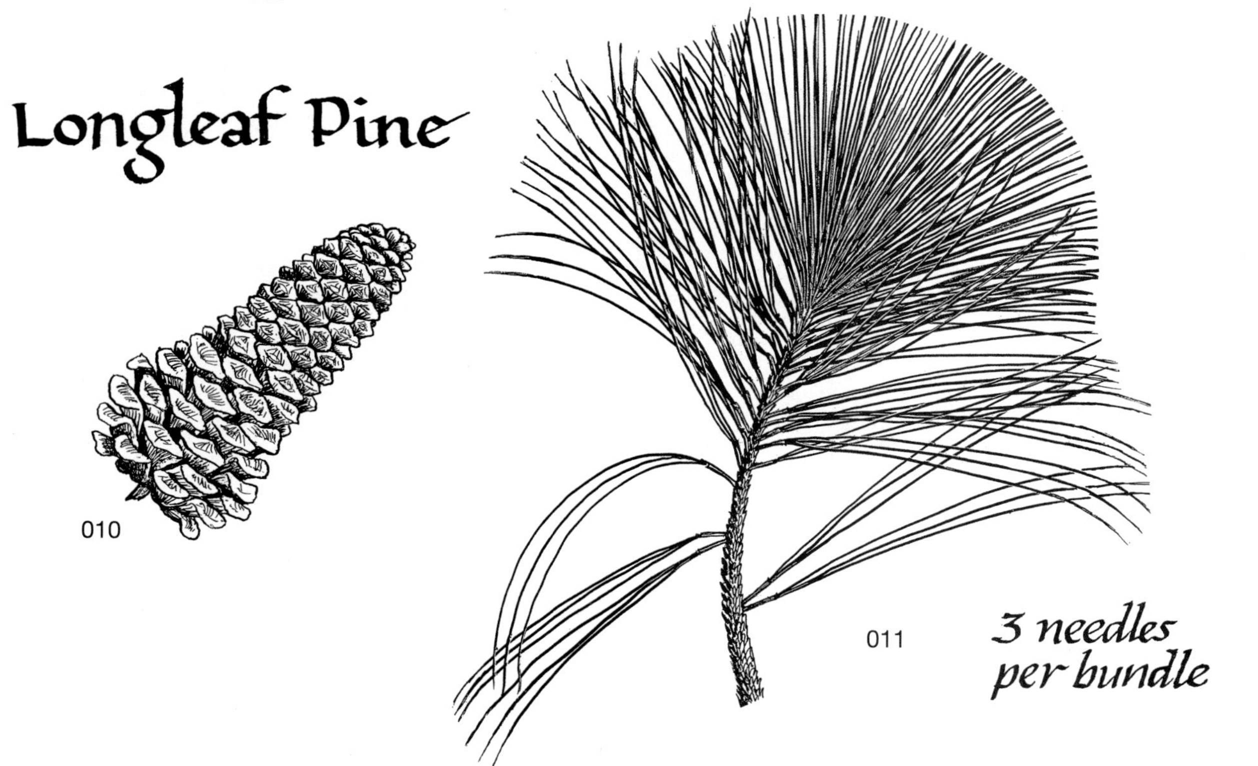

009

Longleaf Pine

010

011

3 needles per bundle

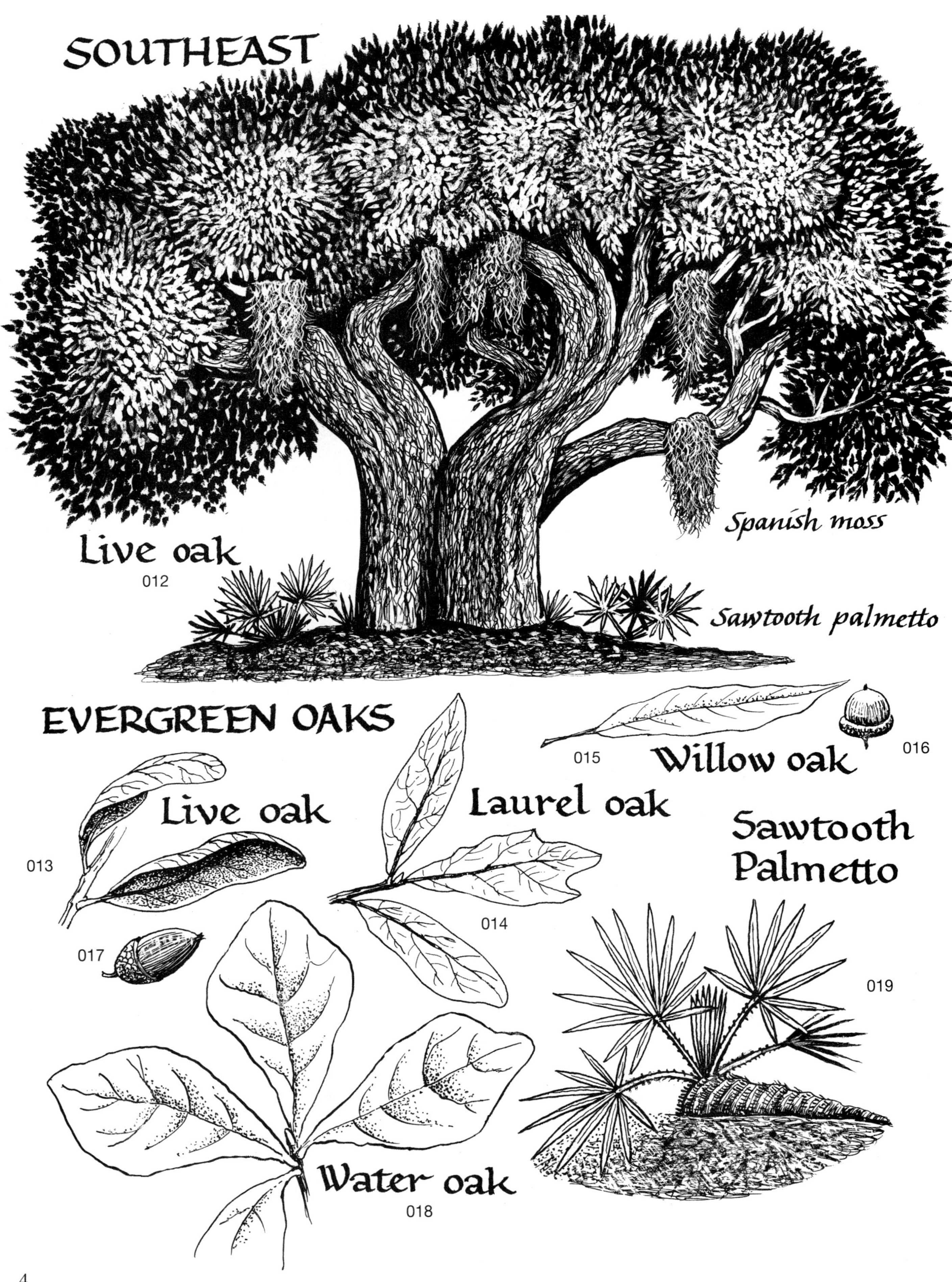
Live oak
012
Spanish moss
Sawtooth palmetto
EVERGREEN OAKS
Live oak
013
017
Laurel oak
014
Water oak
018
015
Willow oak
016
Sawtooth
Palmetto
019

Eastern Deciduous Oaks

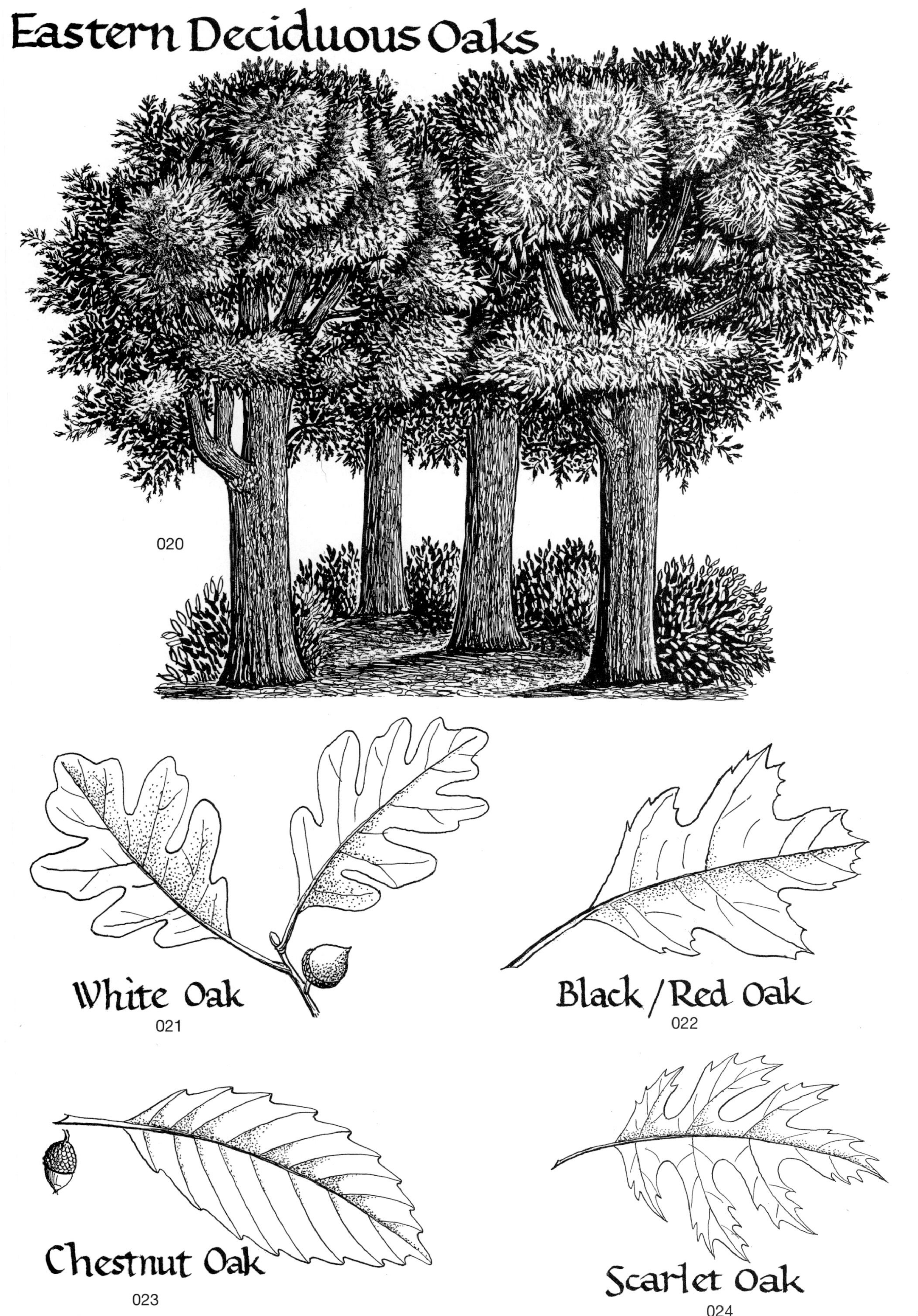

5

EASTERN FOREST Hickory Family

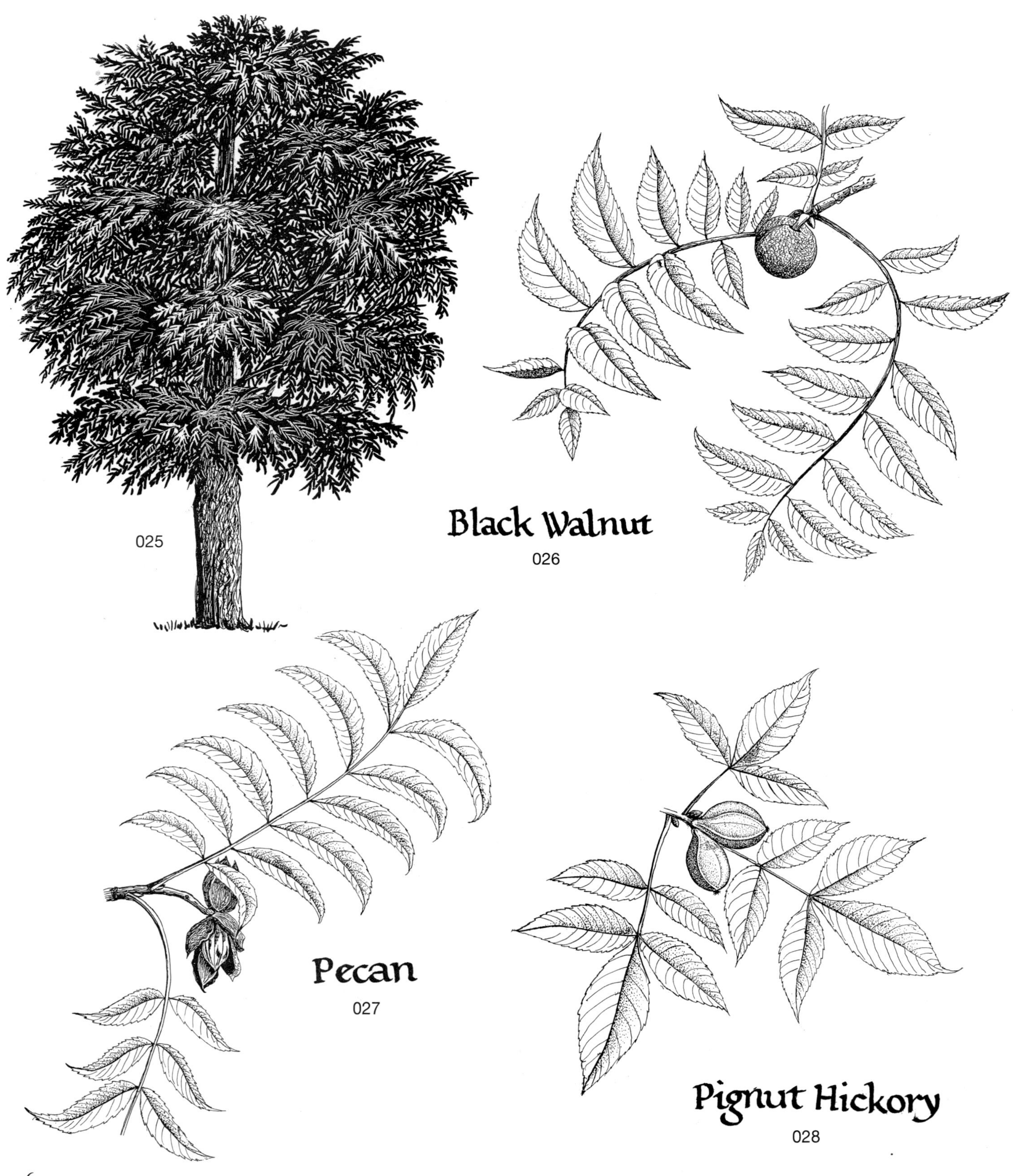

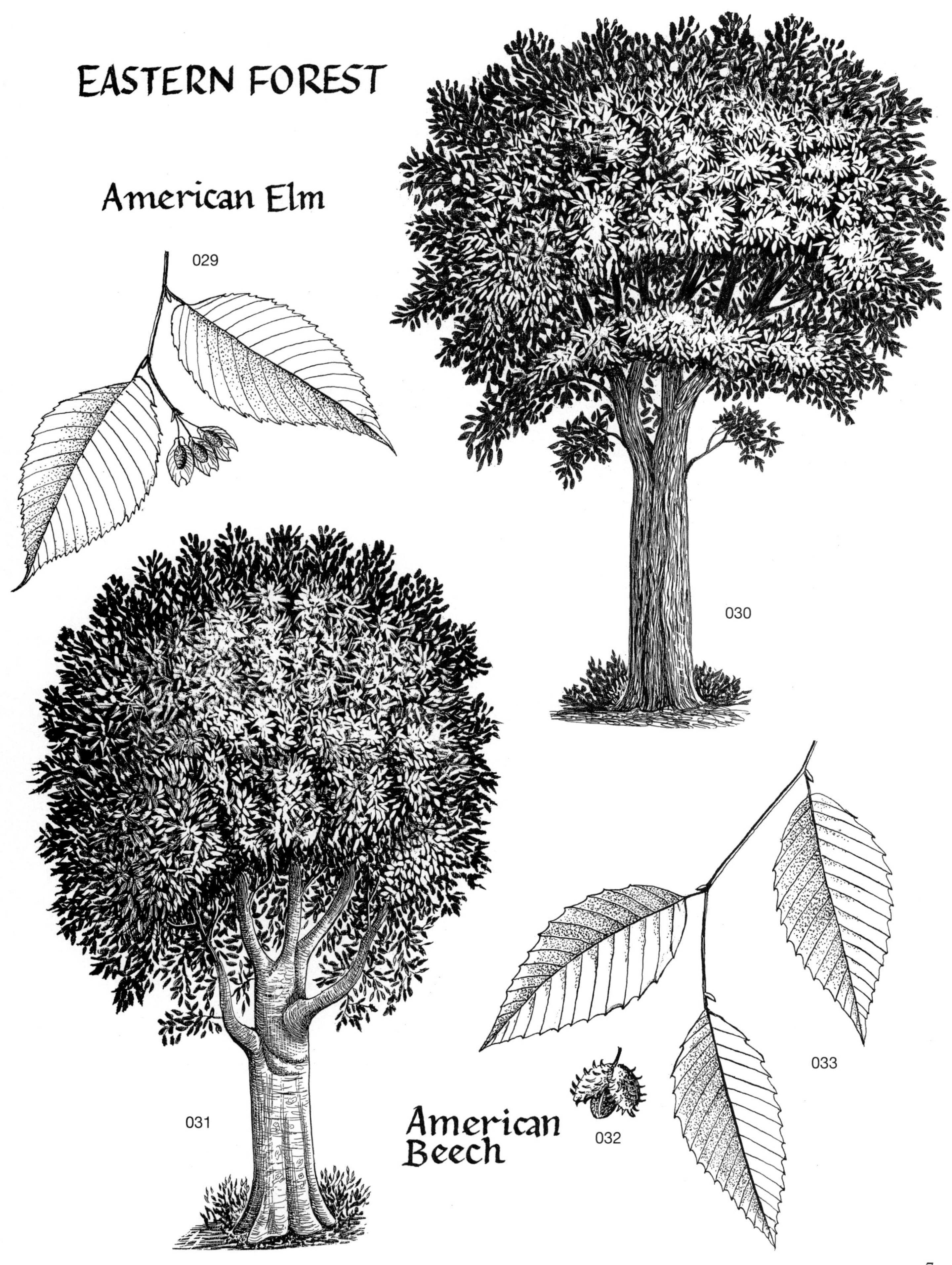

EASTERN FOREST
American Elm
029
030
031
American Beech
032
033

EASTERN FOREST

Sweet Gum

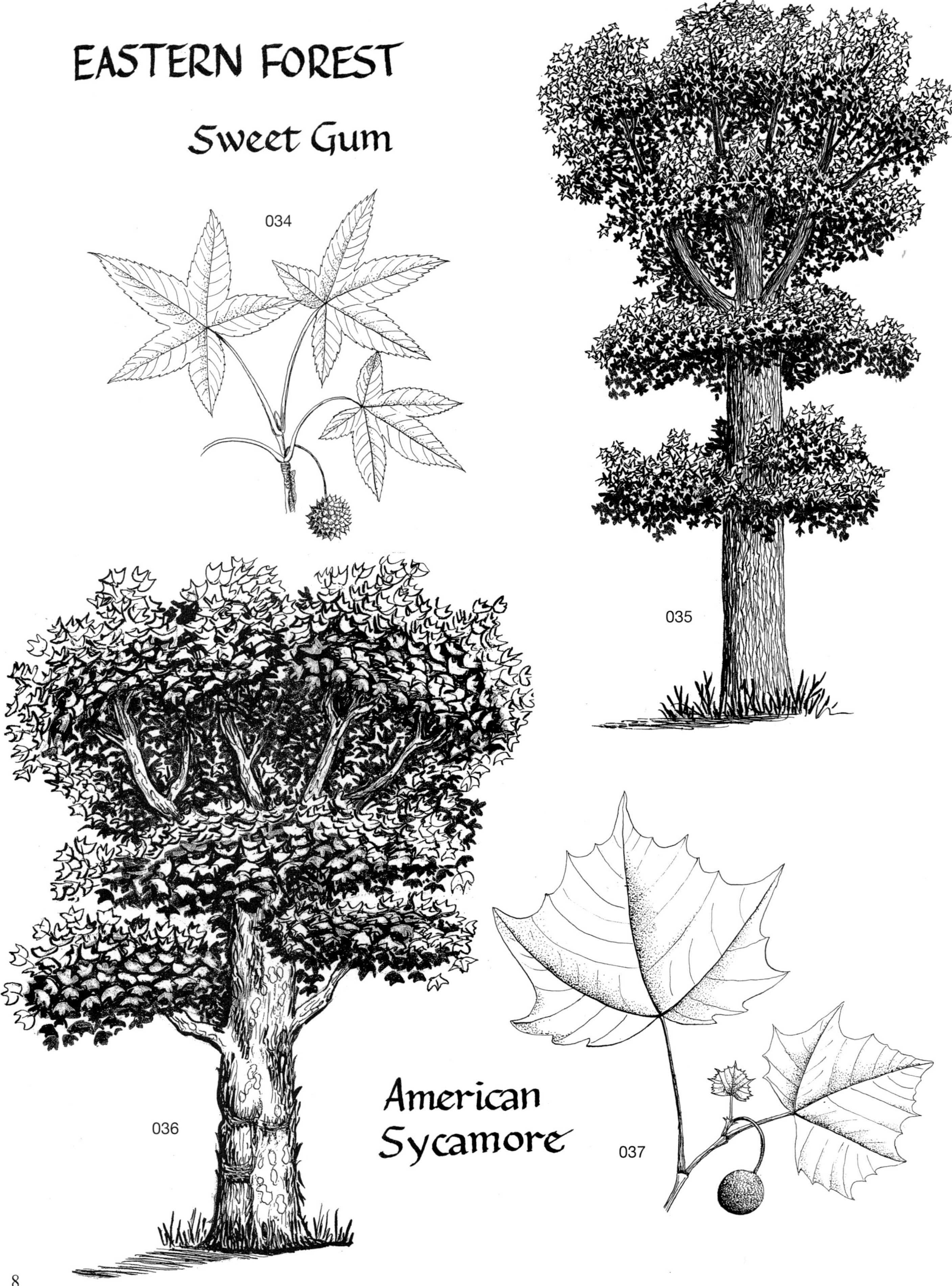

EASTERN FOREST

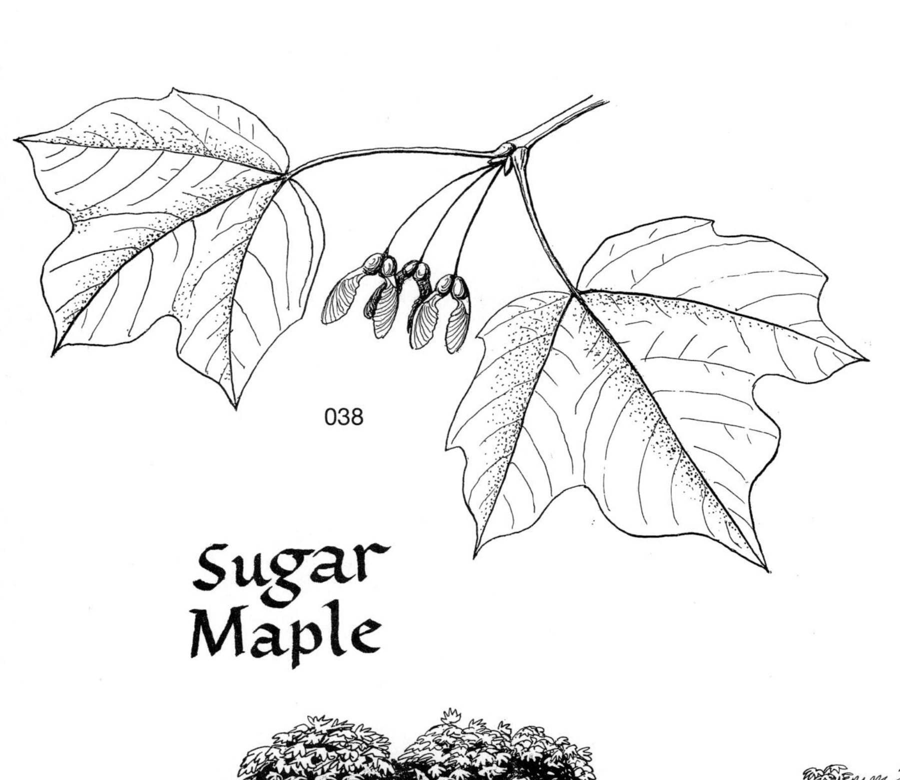

Sugar
Maple

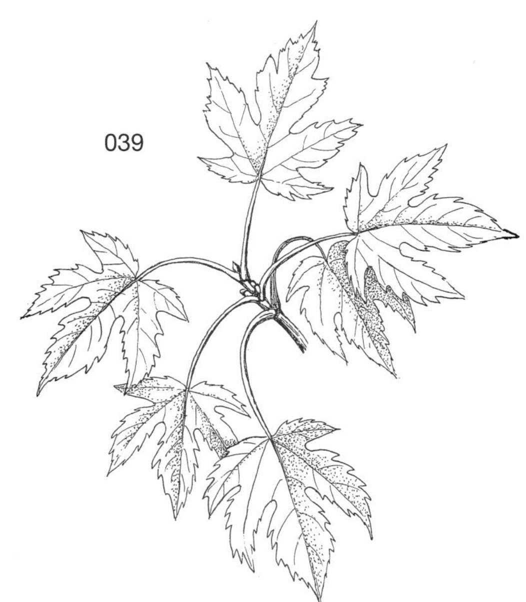

Silver Maple

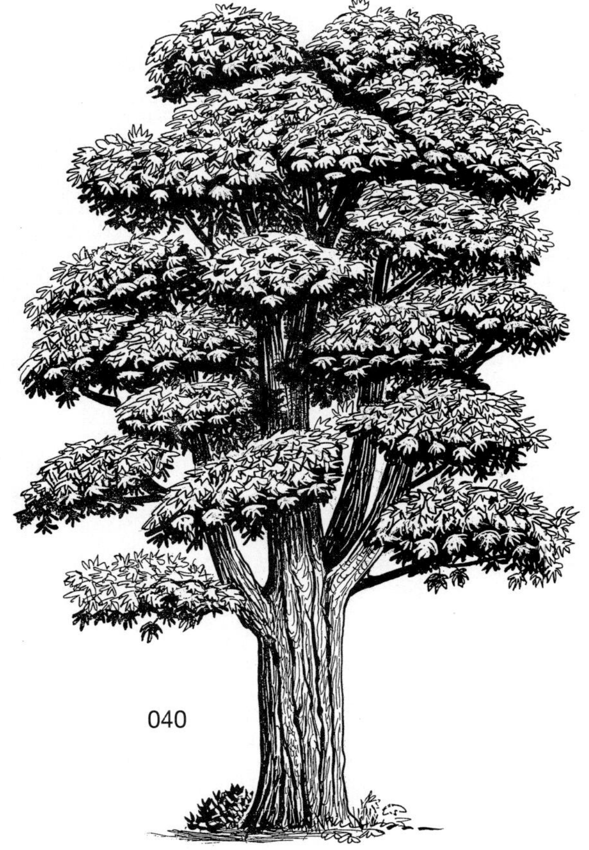

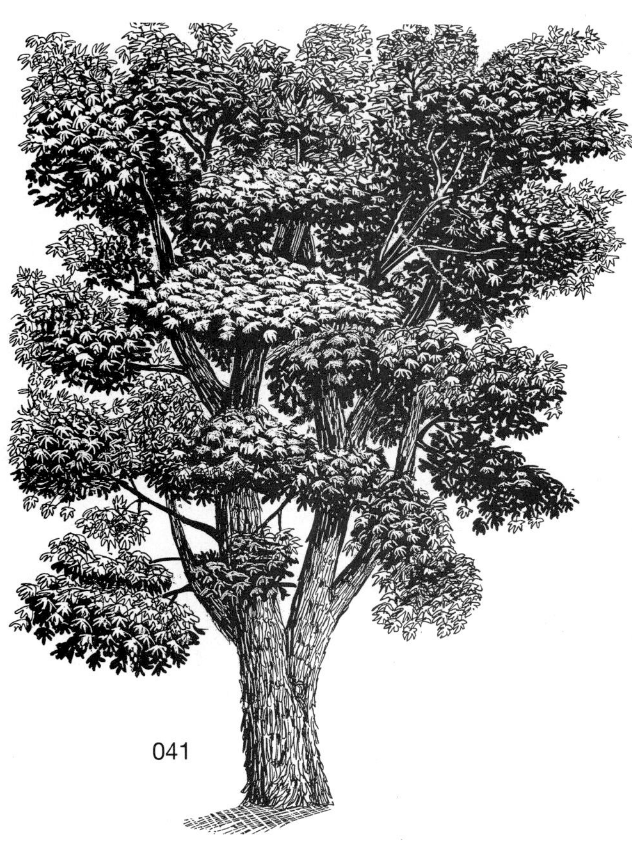

EASTERN FOREST

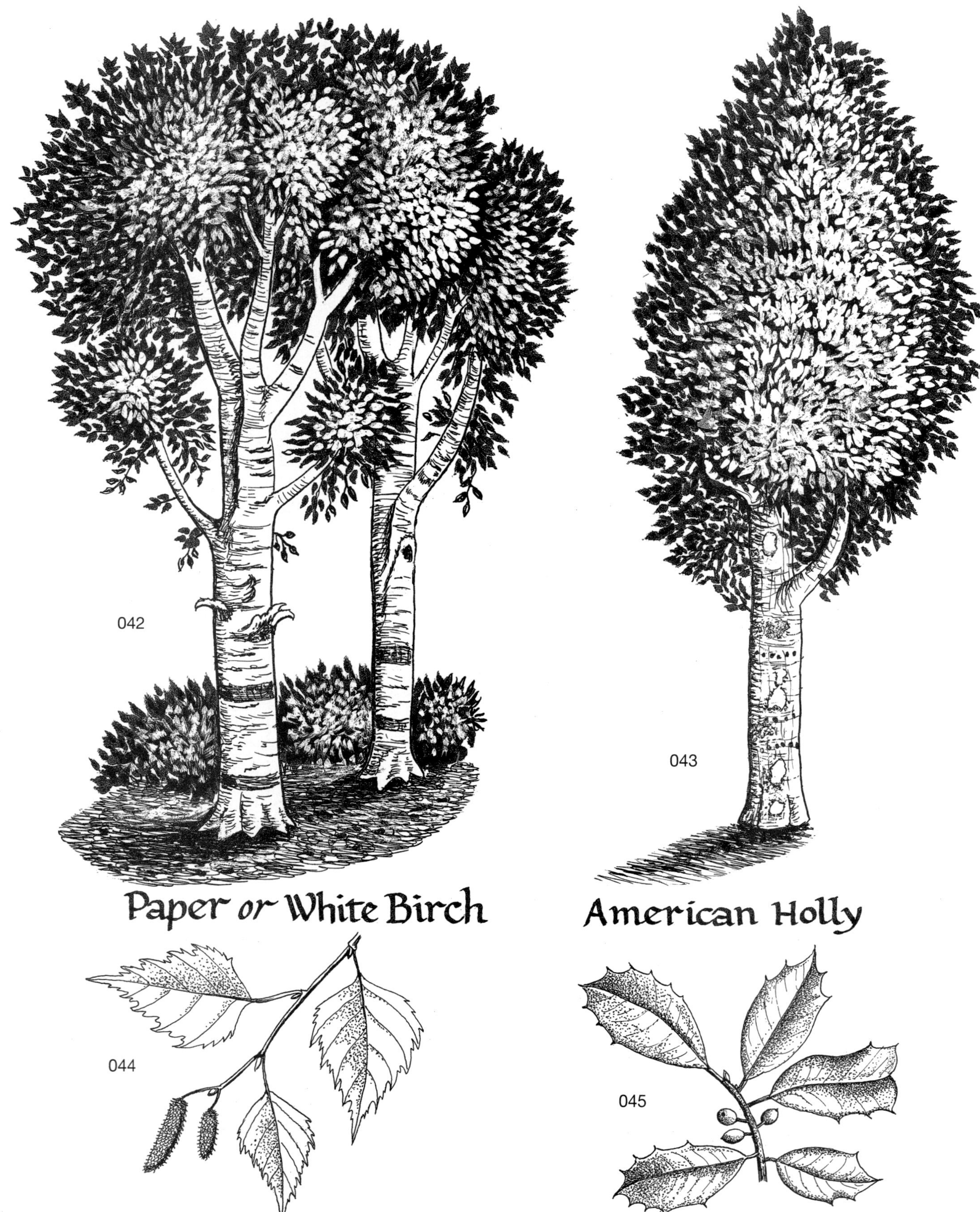

Paper *or* White Birch

American Holly

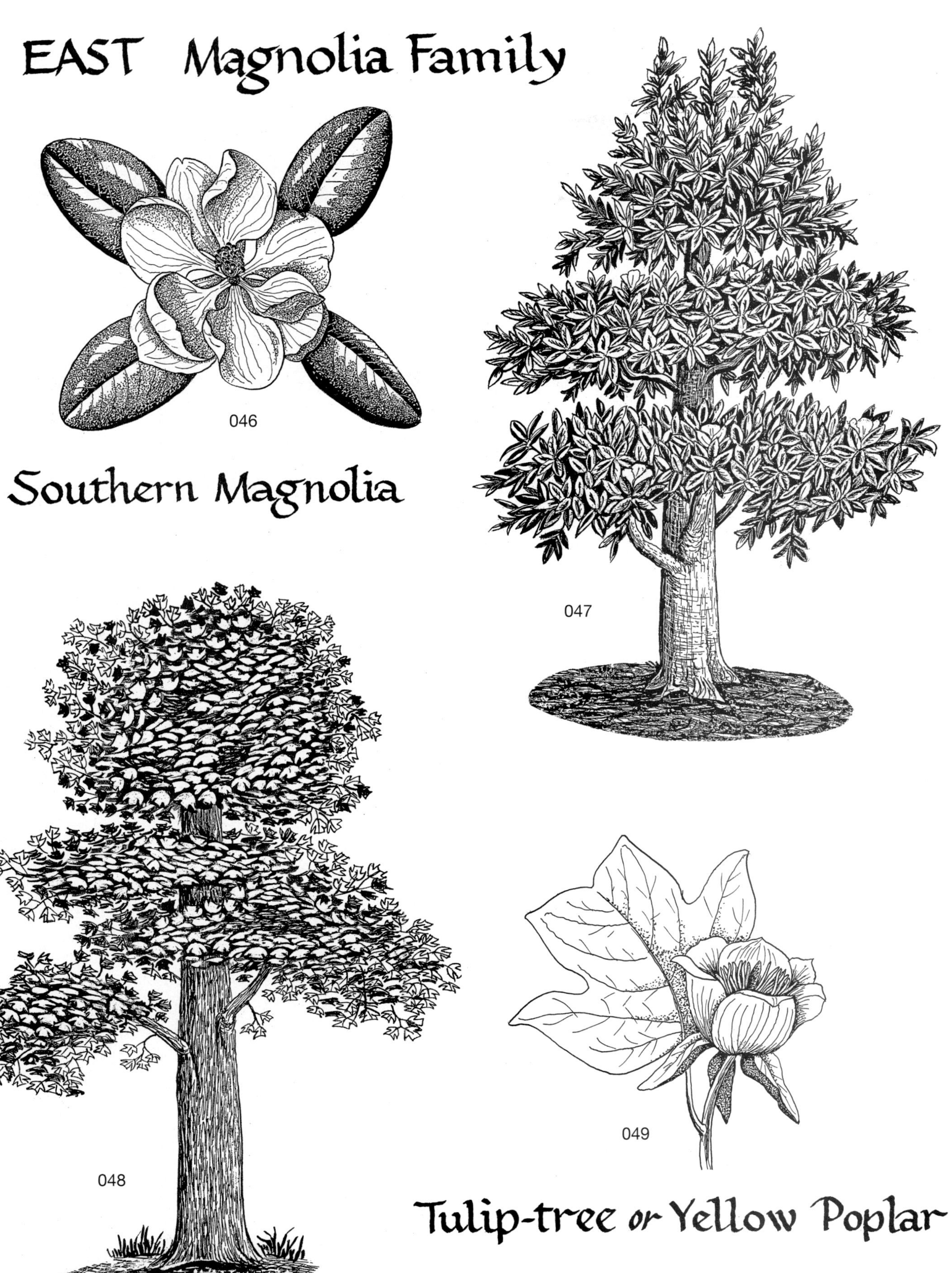

EAST Magnolia Family
046
Southern Magnolia
047
048
049
Tulip-tree or Yellow Poplar

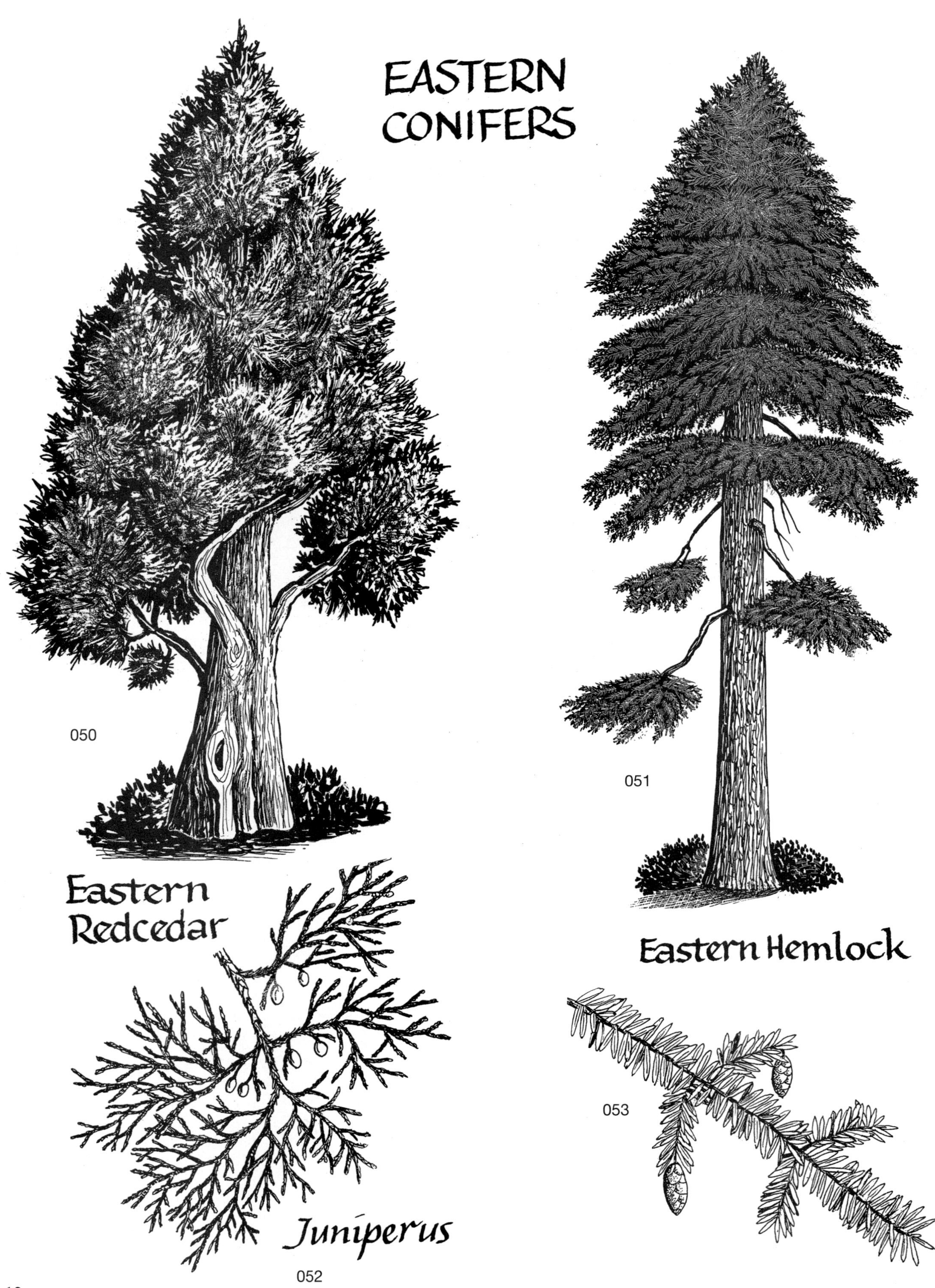

EASTERN CONIFERS
050
Eastern
Redcedar
Juniperus
052
051
Eastern Hemlock
053

EASTERN CONIFERS

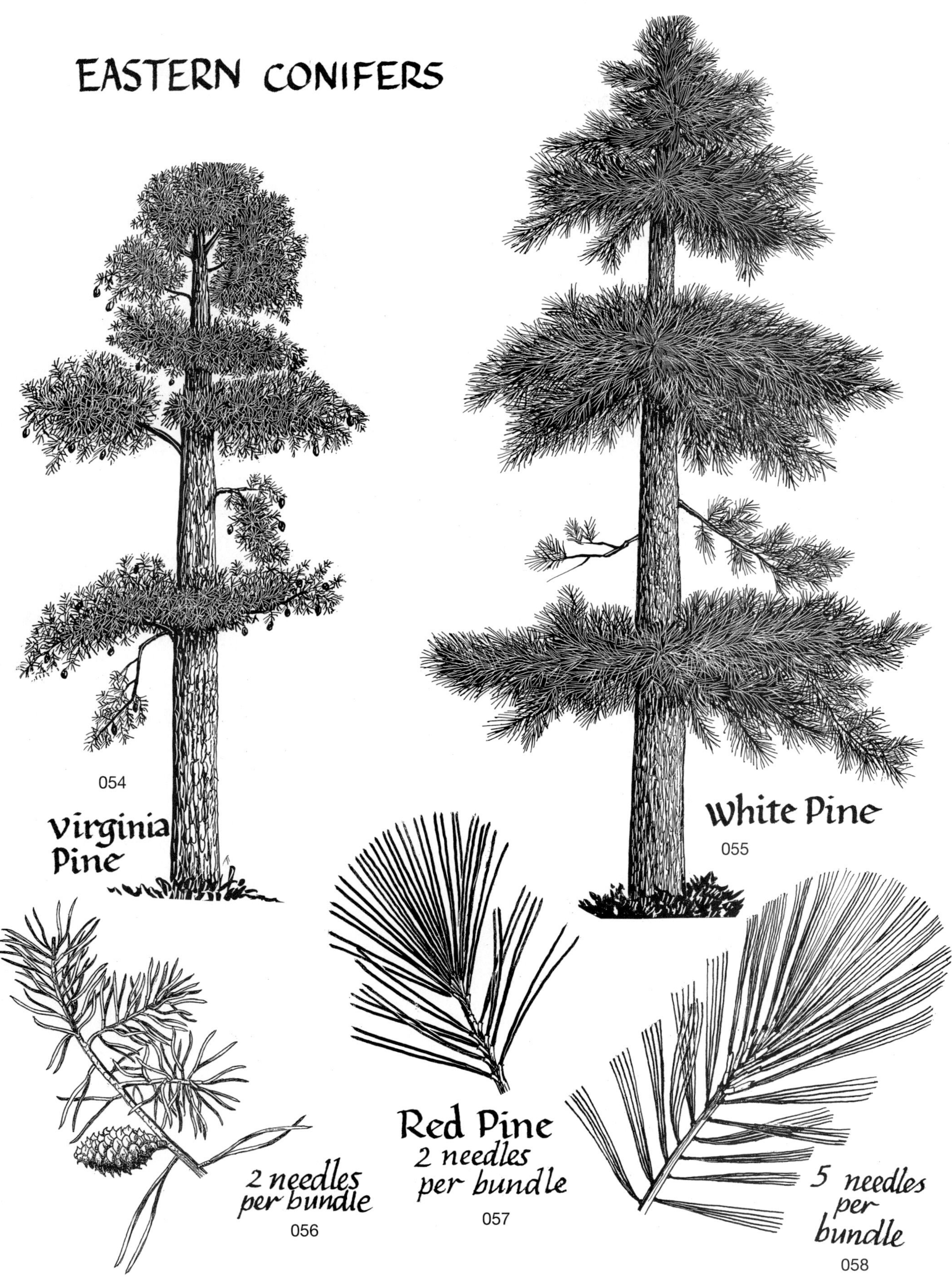

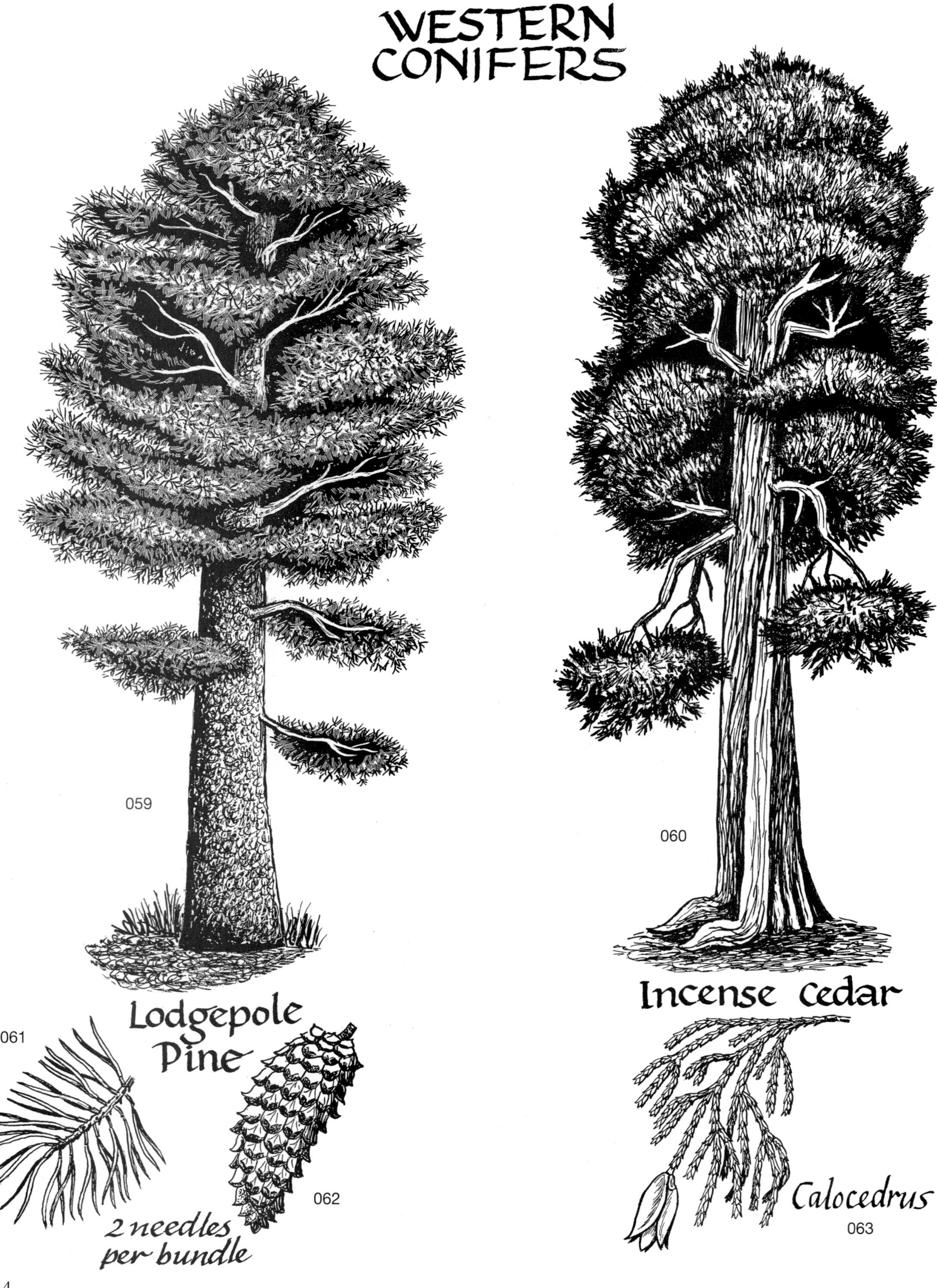

WESTERN
CONIFERS
059
Lodgepole
Pine
061
2 needles
per bundle
062
060
Incense cedar
Calocedrus
063

WESTERN CONIFERS

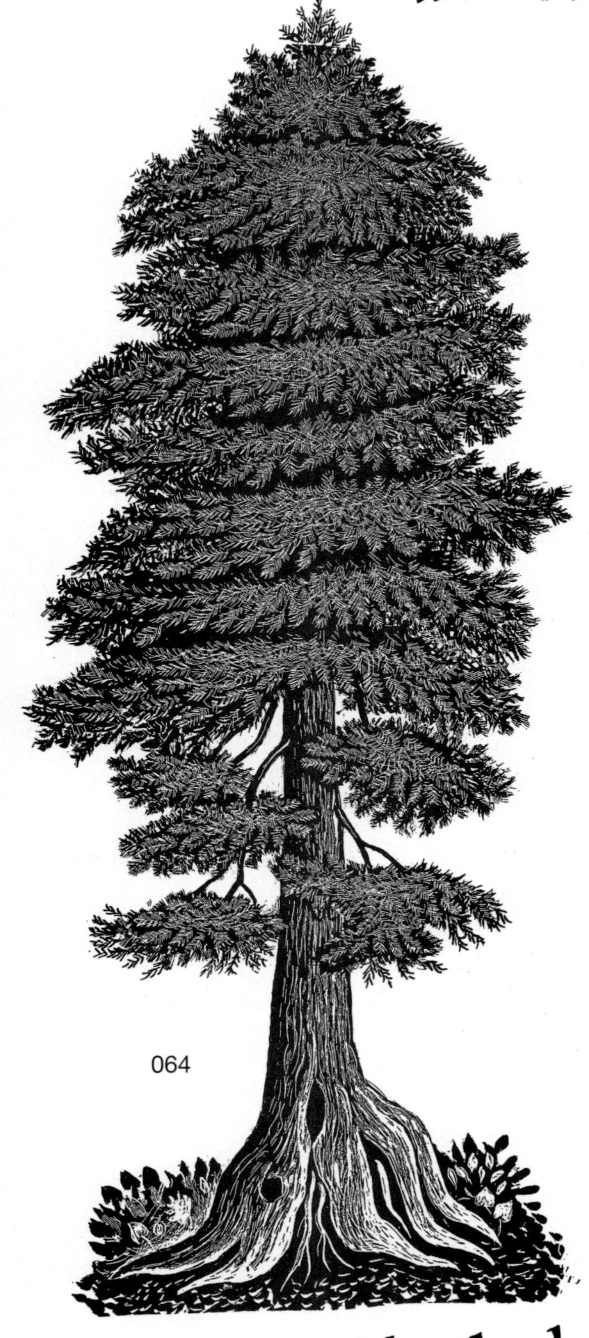

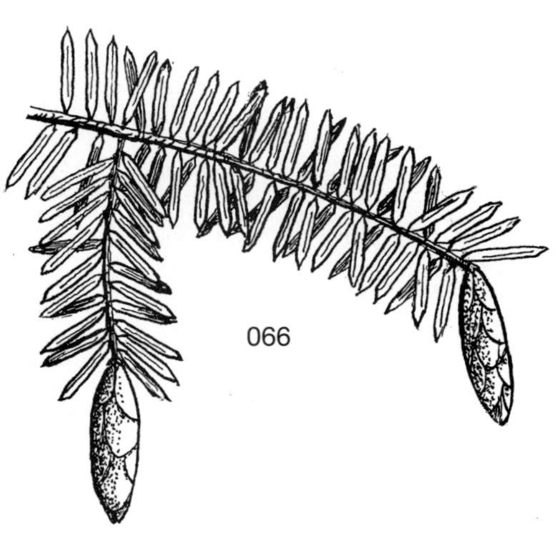

Western Hemlock

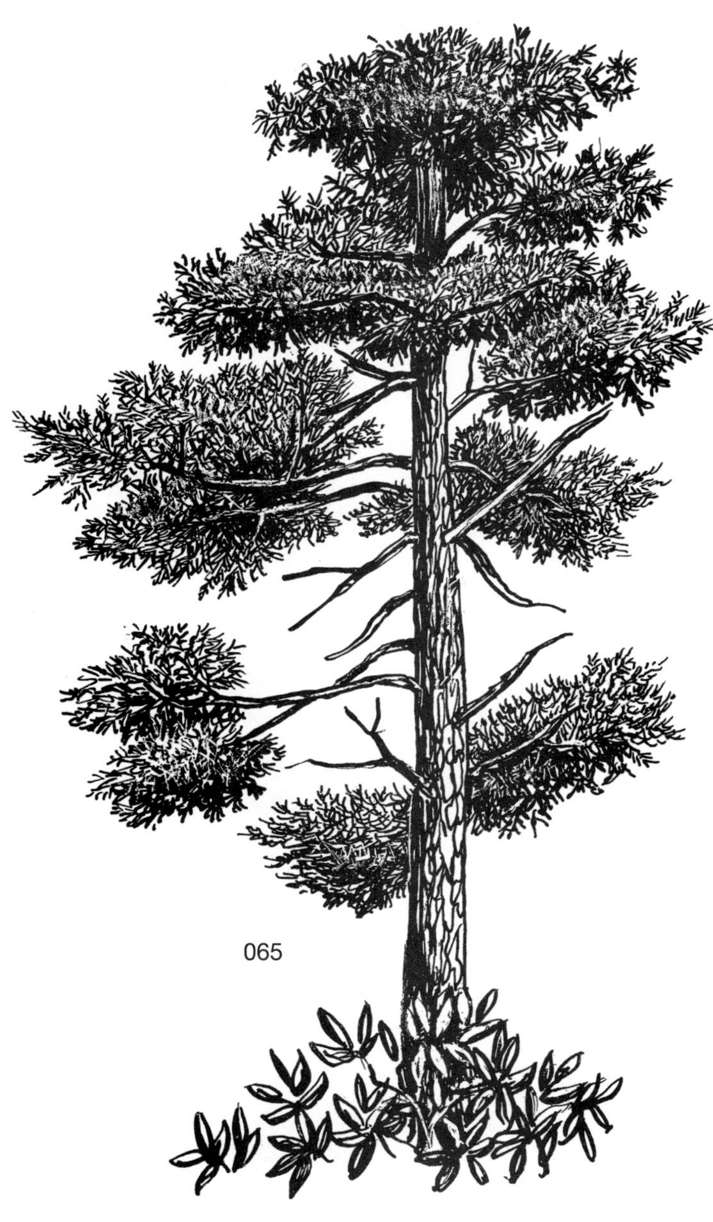

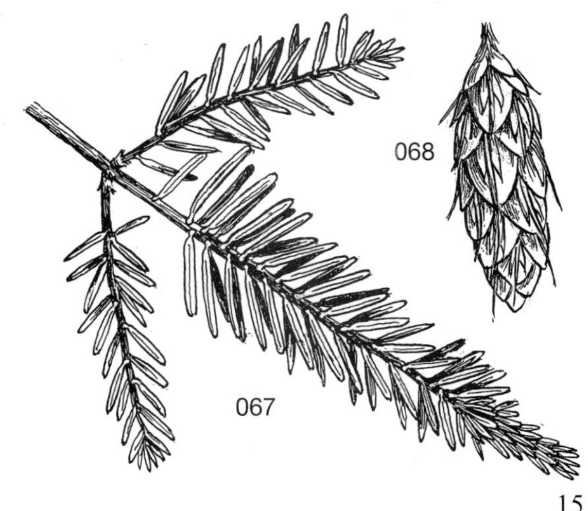

Douglas Fir

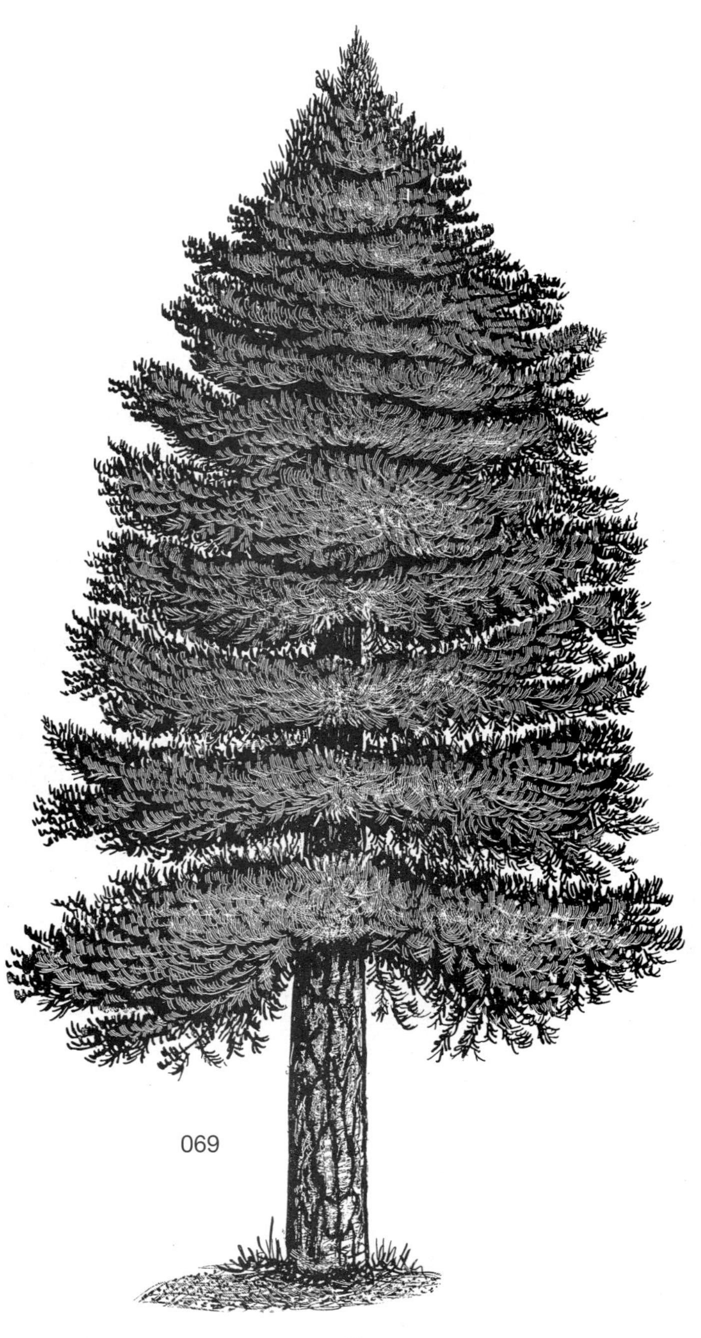

069

White Fir

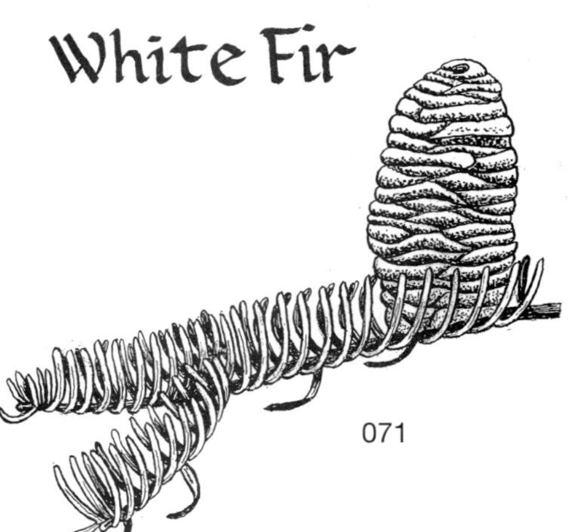

071

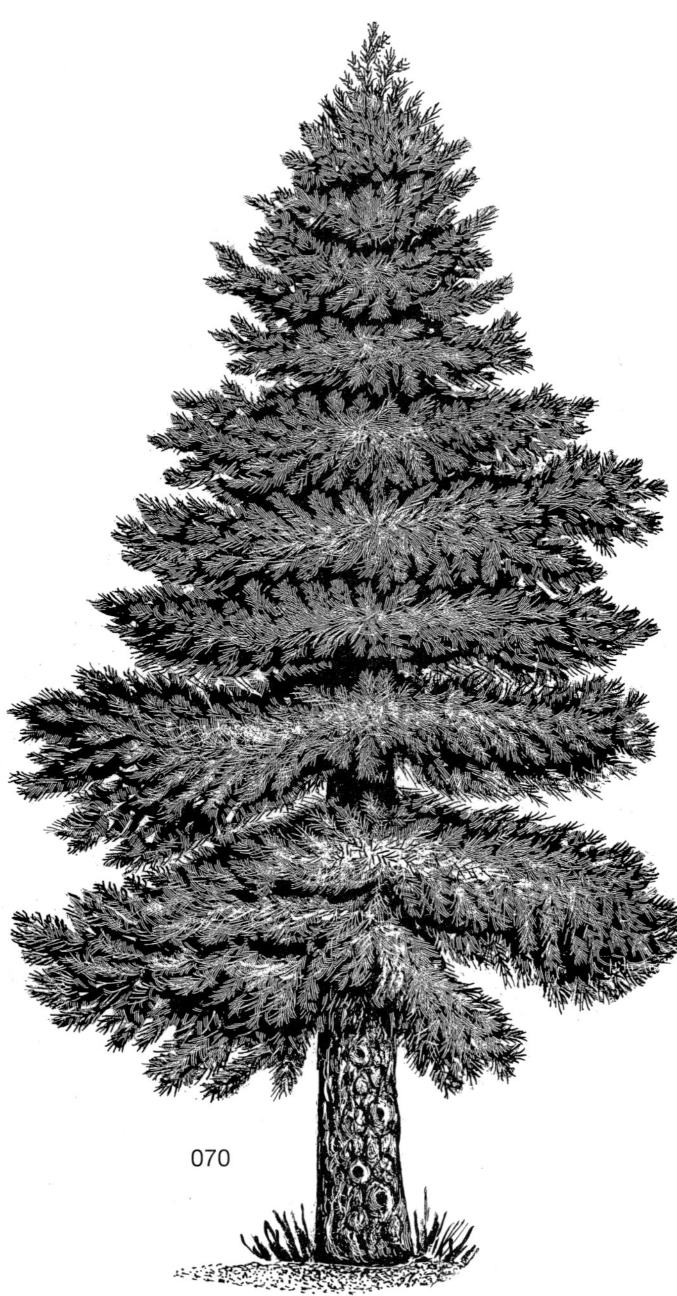

070

Blue Spruce

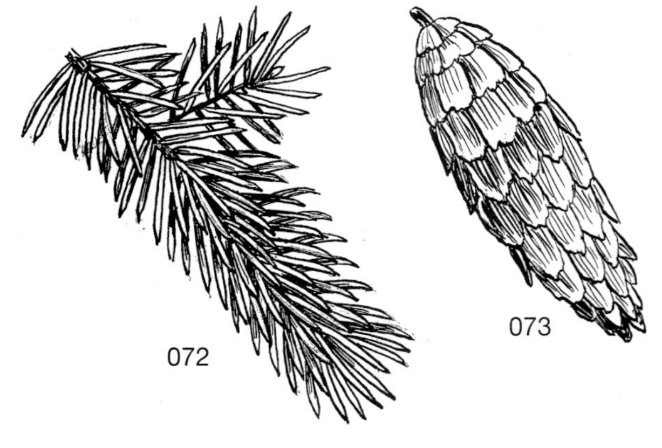

072

073

WESTERN PINES

Ponderosa Pine

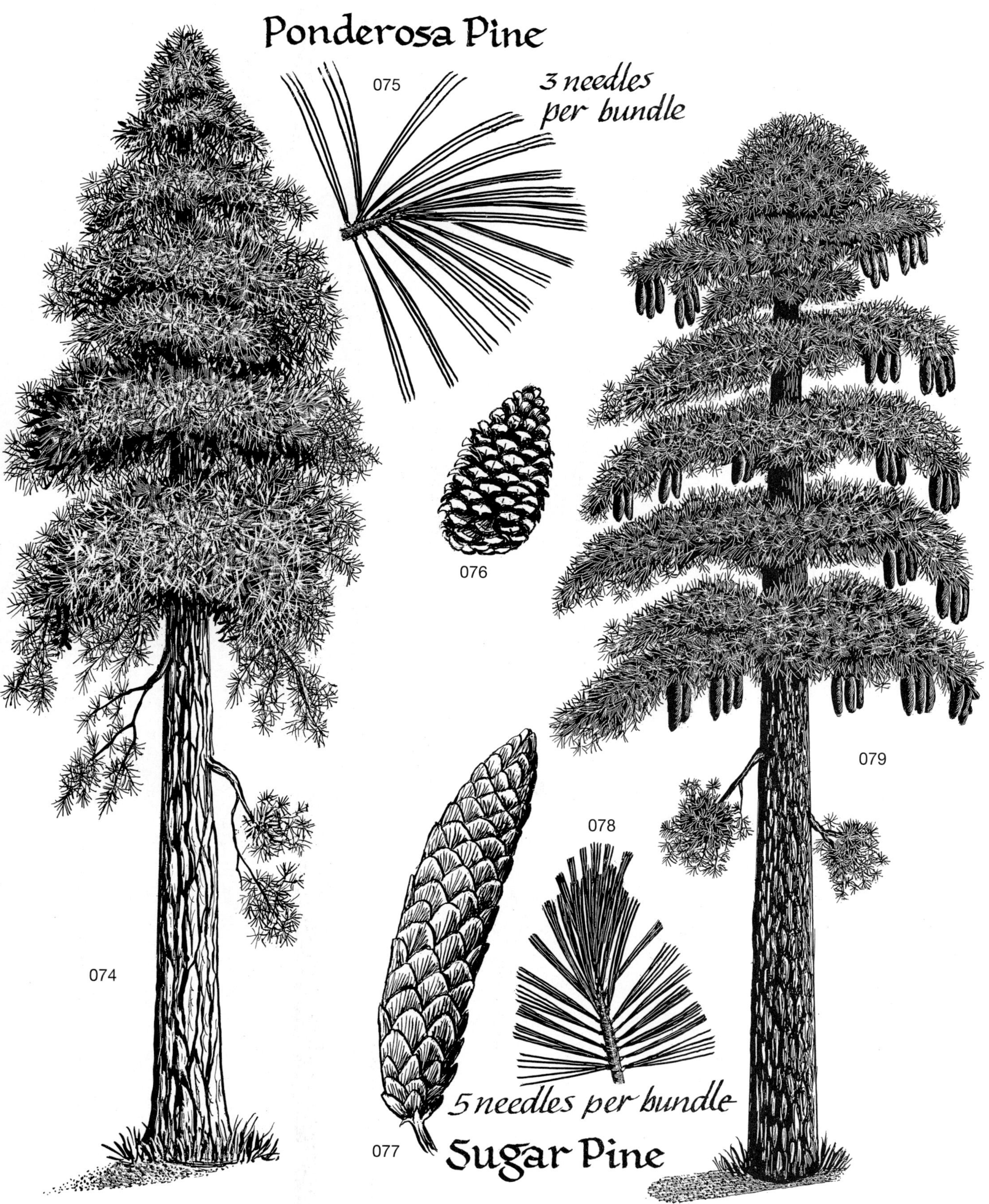

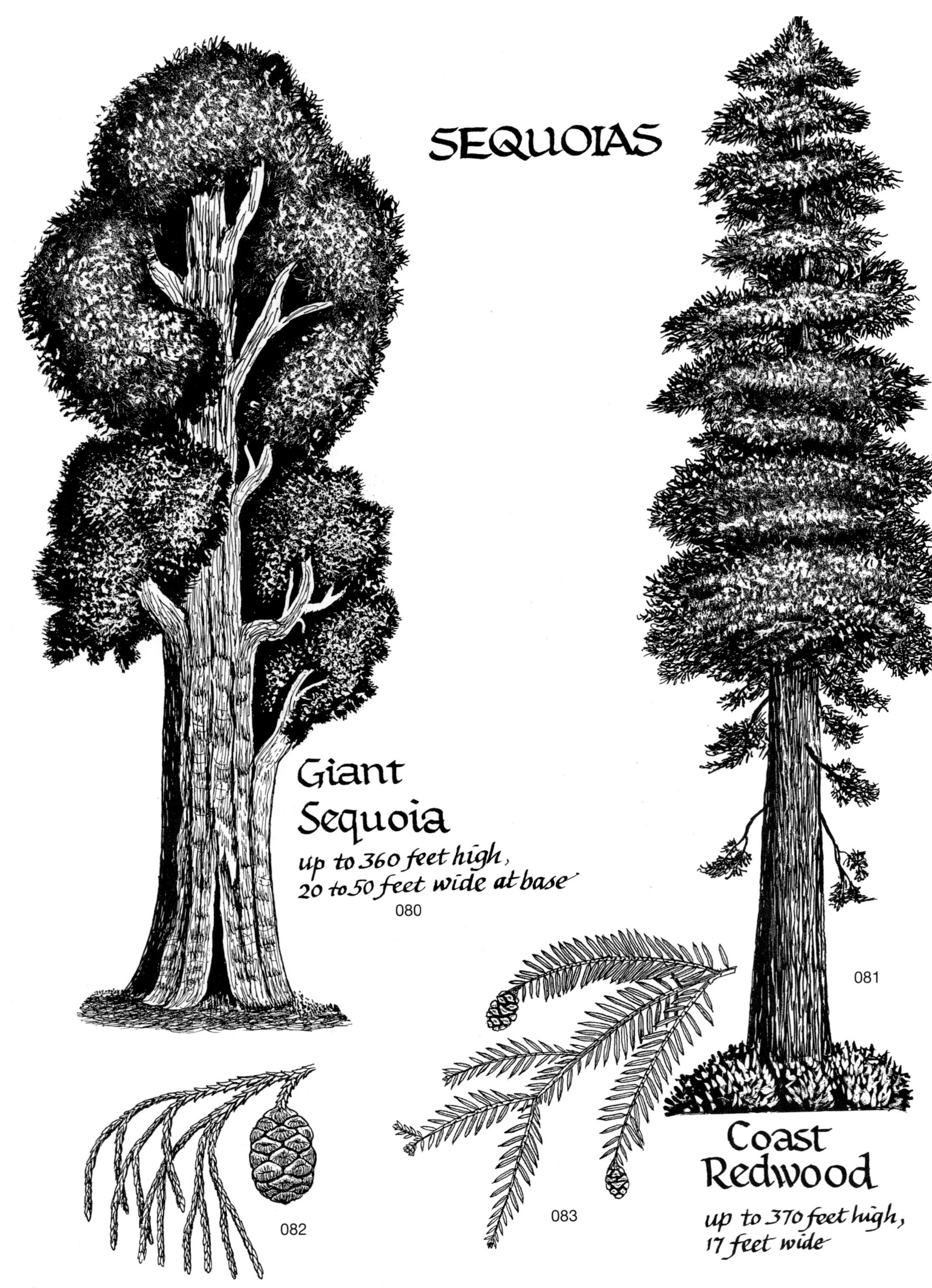

SEQUOIAS
Giant
Sequoia
up to 360 feet high,
20 to 50 feet wide at base
080
081
082
083
Coast
Redwood
up to 370 feet high,
17 feet wide

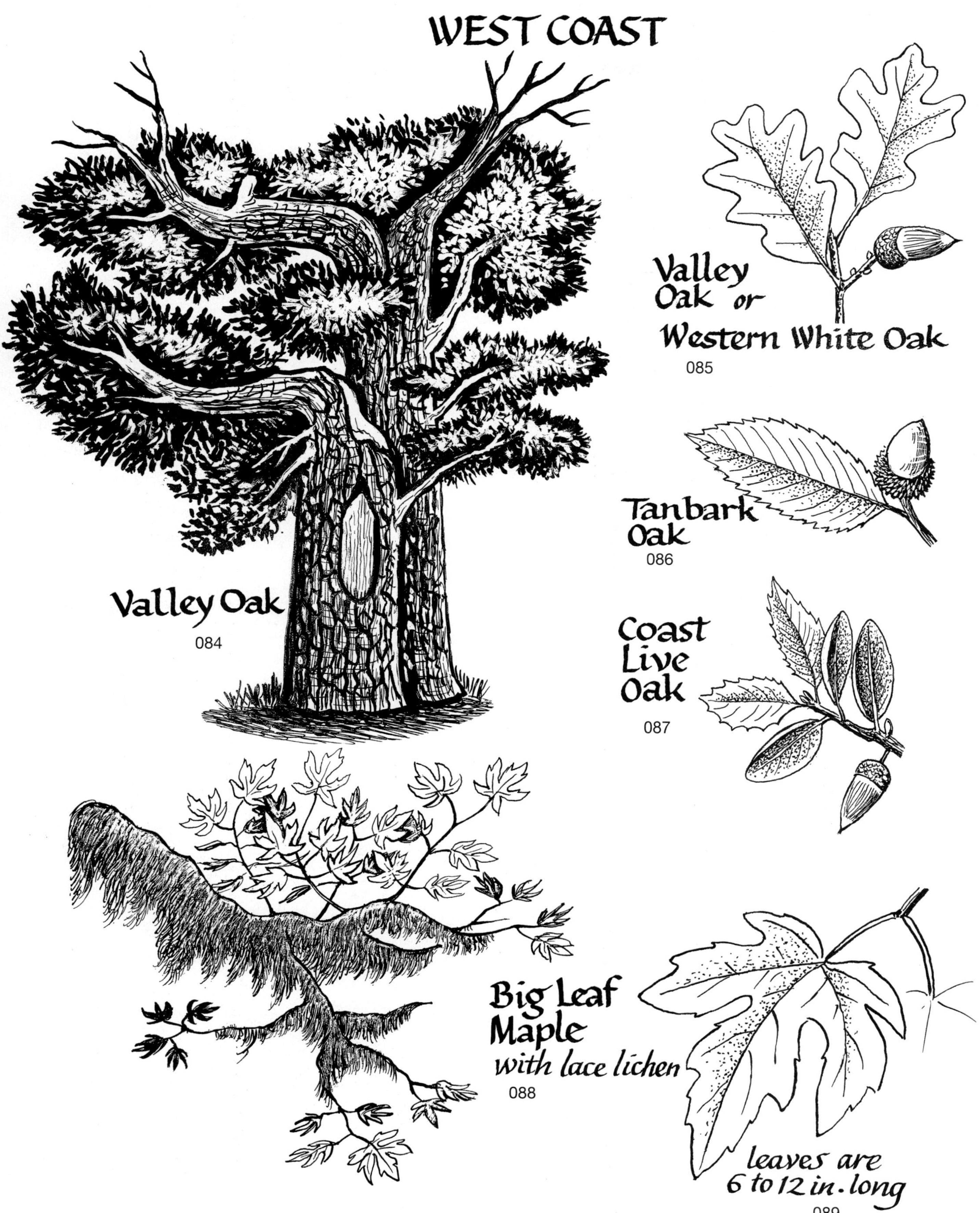

WEST COAST
Valley Oak or Western White Oak
085
Tanbark Oak
086
Coast Live Oak
087
Valley Oak
084
Big Leaf Maple
with lace lichen
088
leaves are 6 to 12 in. long
089

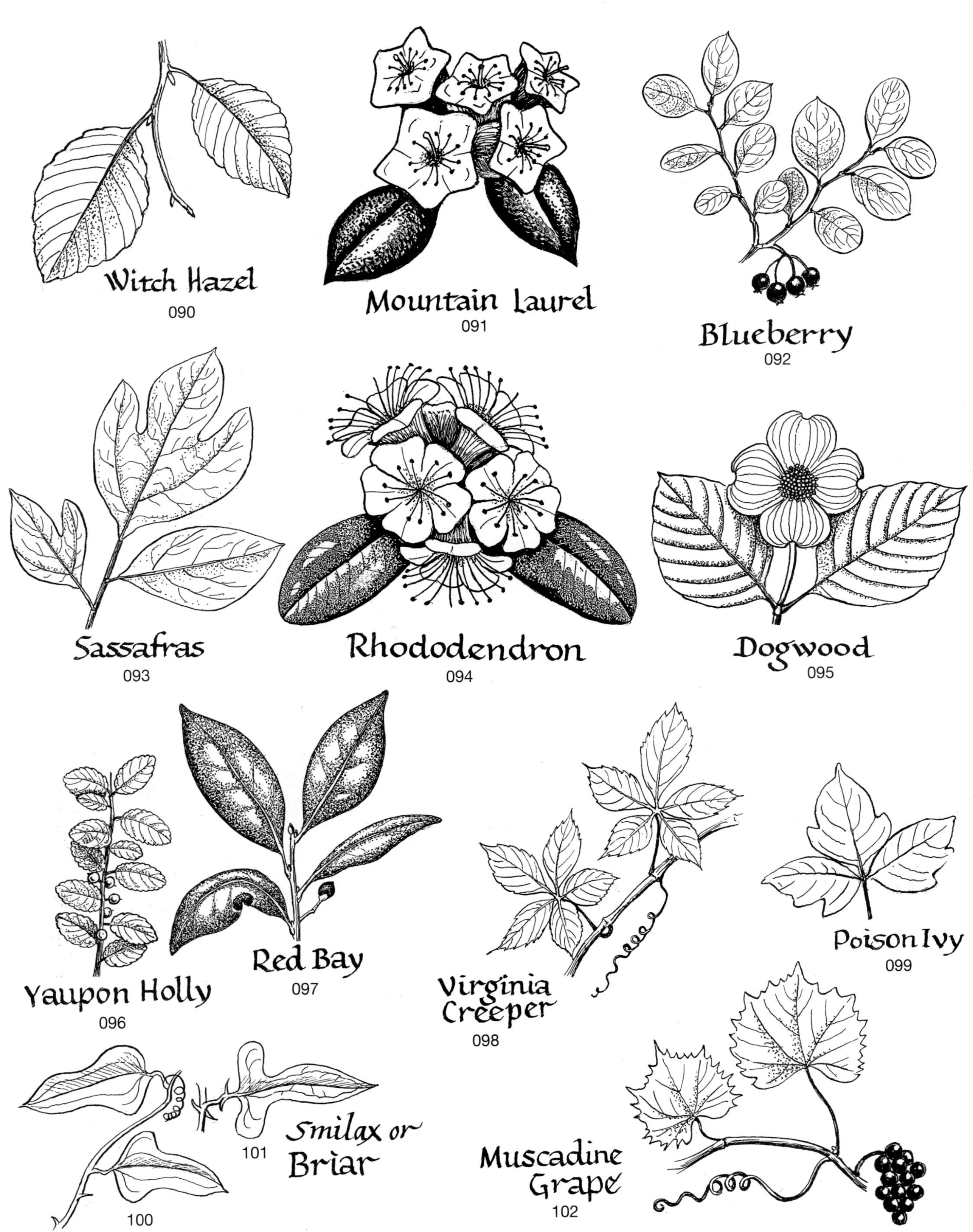

Witch Hazel
090

Mountain Laurel
091

Blueberry
092

Sassafras
093

Rhododendron
094

Dogwood
095

Yaupon Holly
096

Red Bay
097

Virginia Creeper
098

Poison Ivy
099

Smilax or Briar
101

100

Muscadine Grape
102

Forest shrubs, small trees & vines

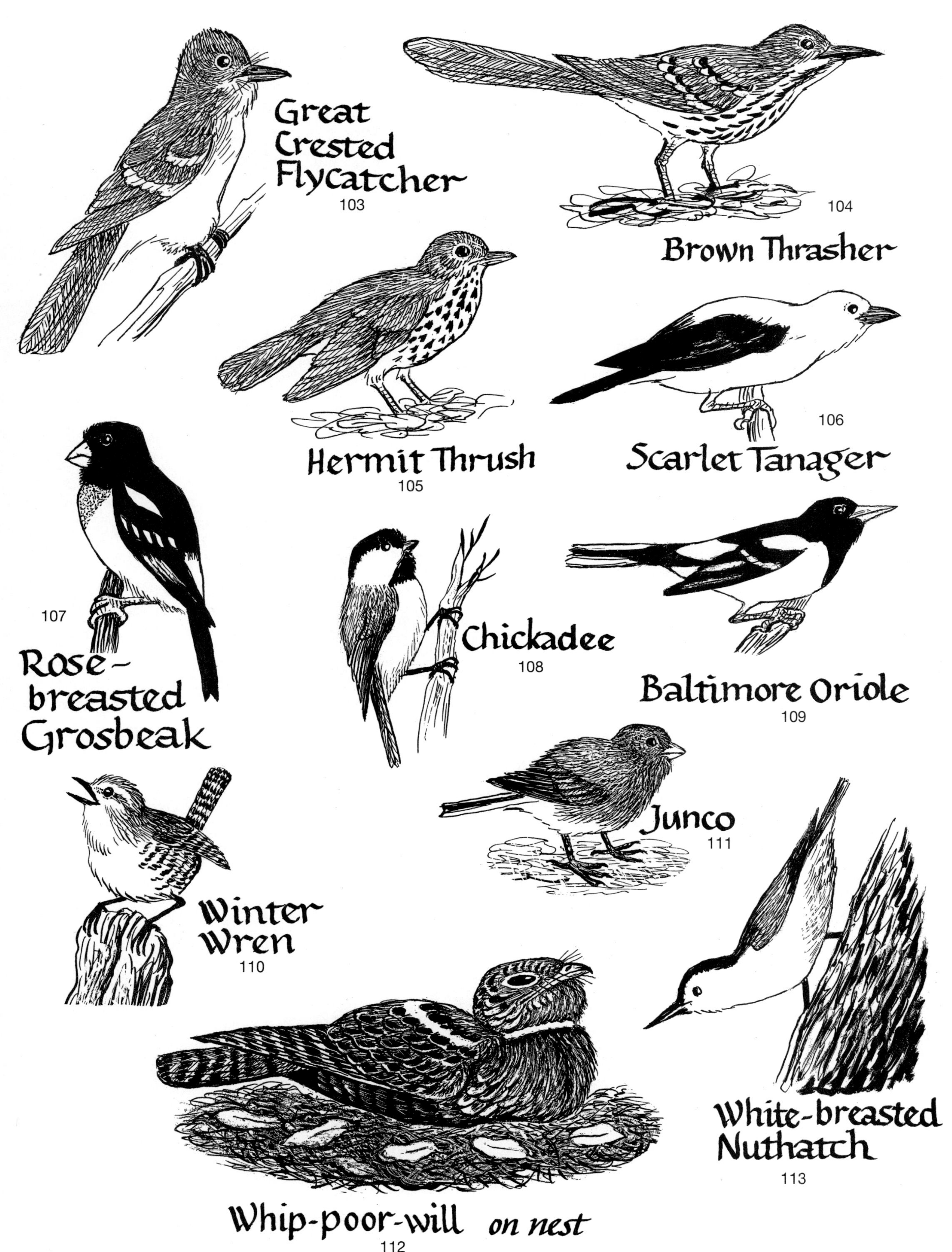

Great Crested Flycatcher
103
Brown Thrasher
104
Hermit Thrush
105
Scarlet Tanager
106
Rose-breasted Grosbeak
107
Chickadee
108
Baltimore Oriole
109
Junco
111
Winter Wren
110
White-breasted Nuthatch
113
Whip-poor-will on nest
112

Raven
114
Crow
115
Steller's
Jay
116
Gray
Jay
117
Clark's
Nutcracker
118
Blue Jay
119
Crow Family

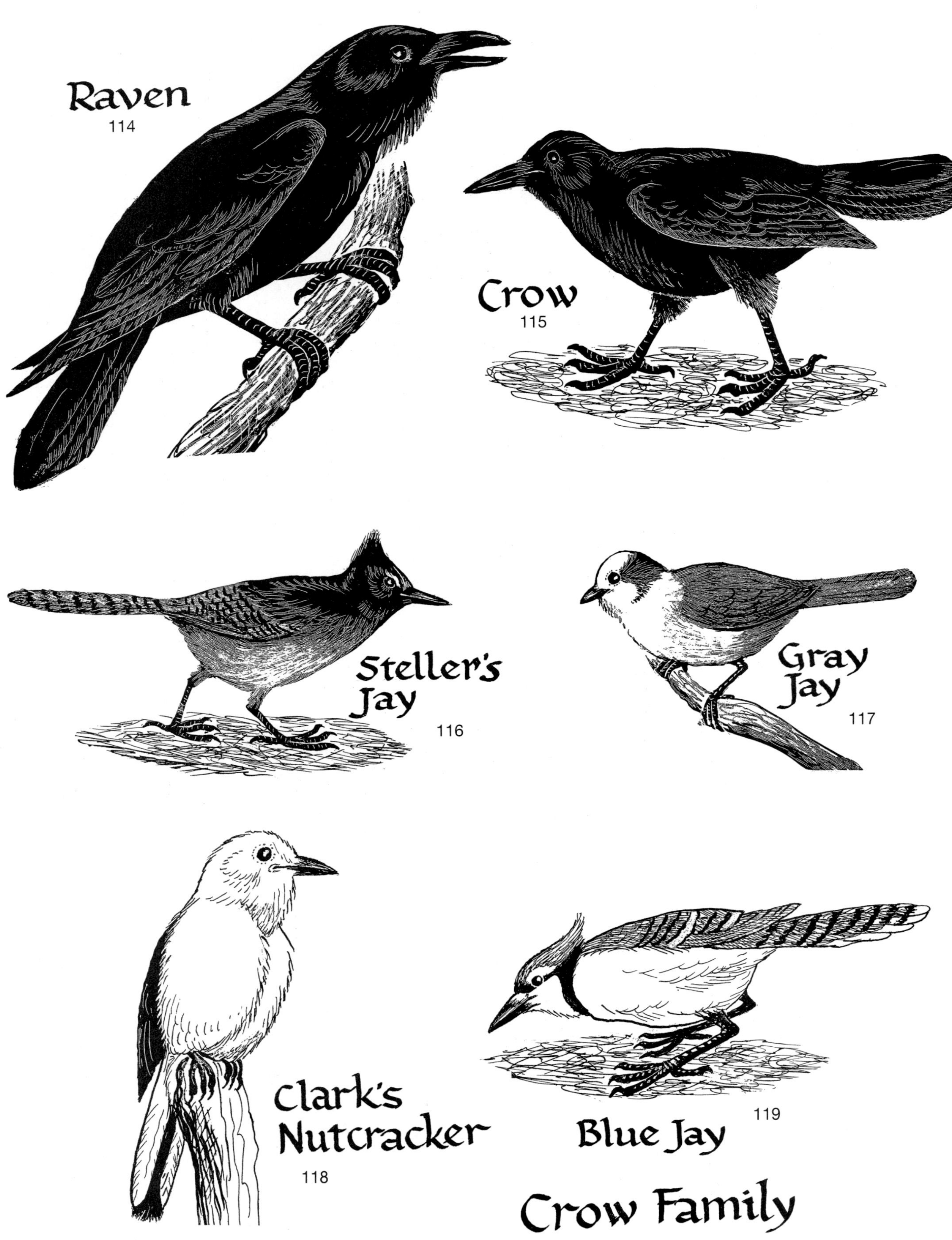

22

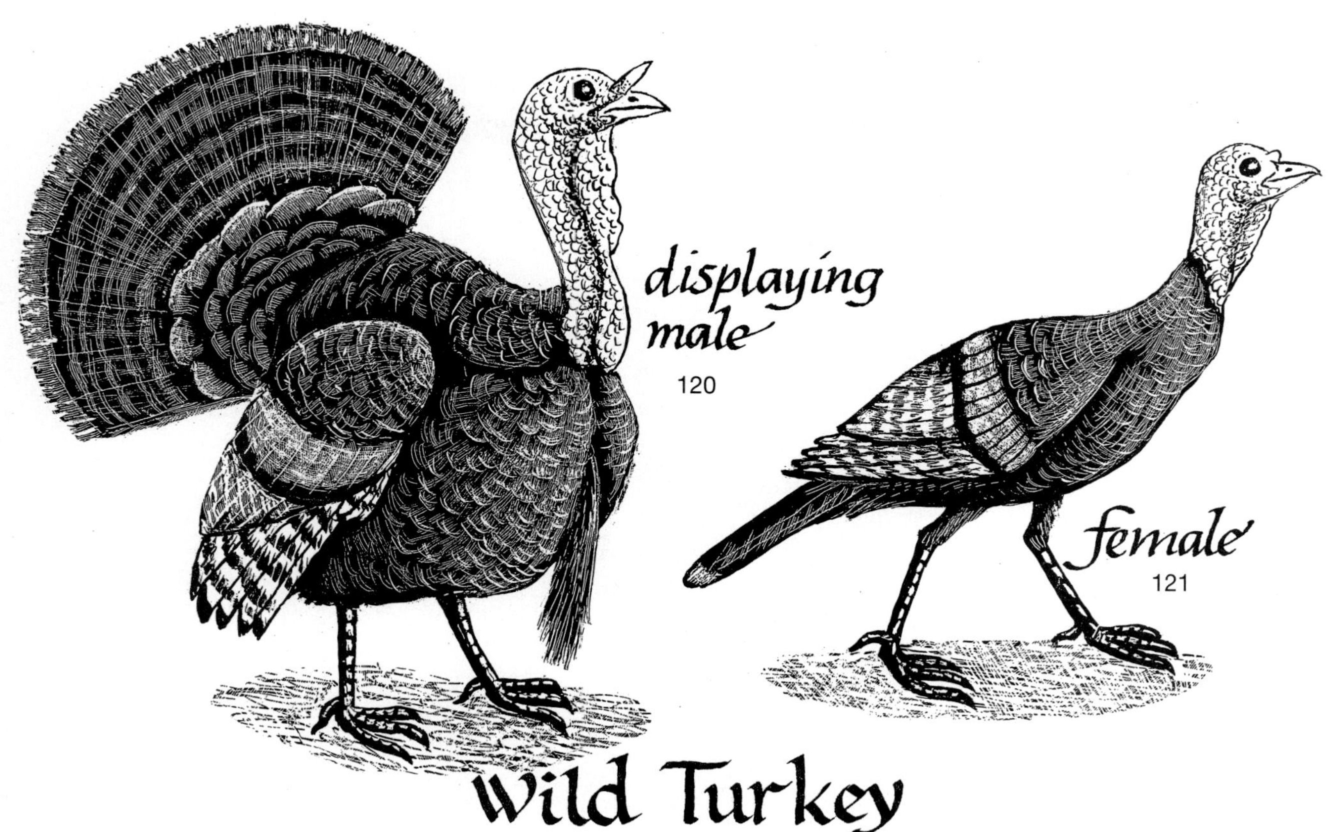

Wild Turkey

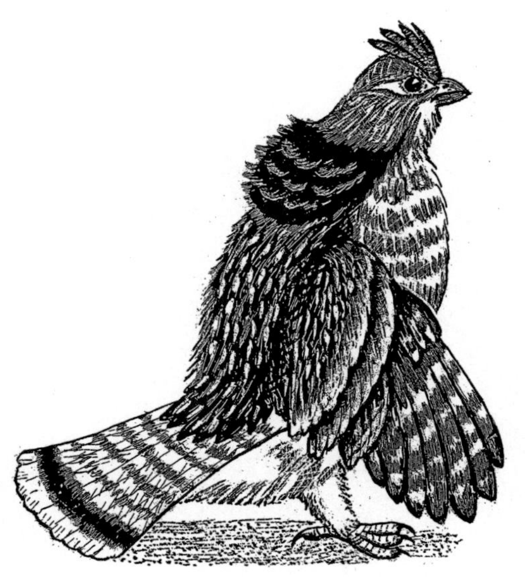

Ruffed Grouse

122

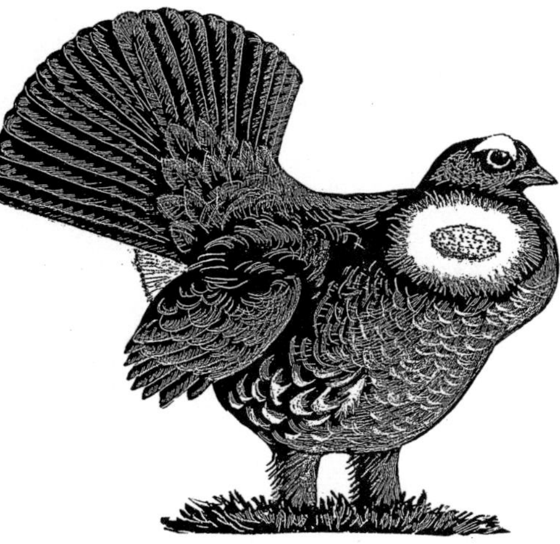

Blue Grouse

123

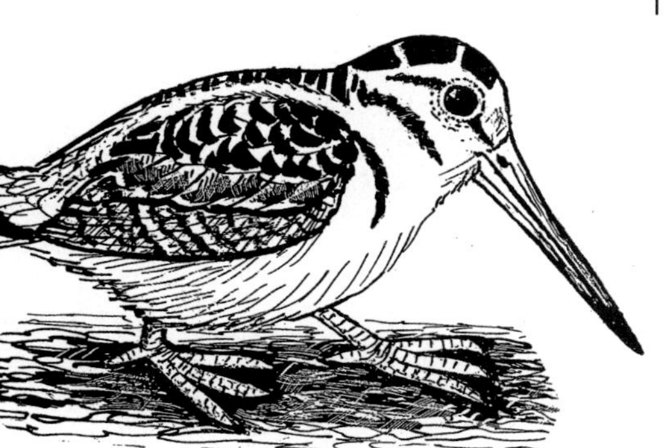

Woodcock

124

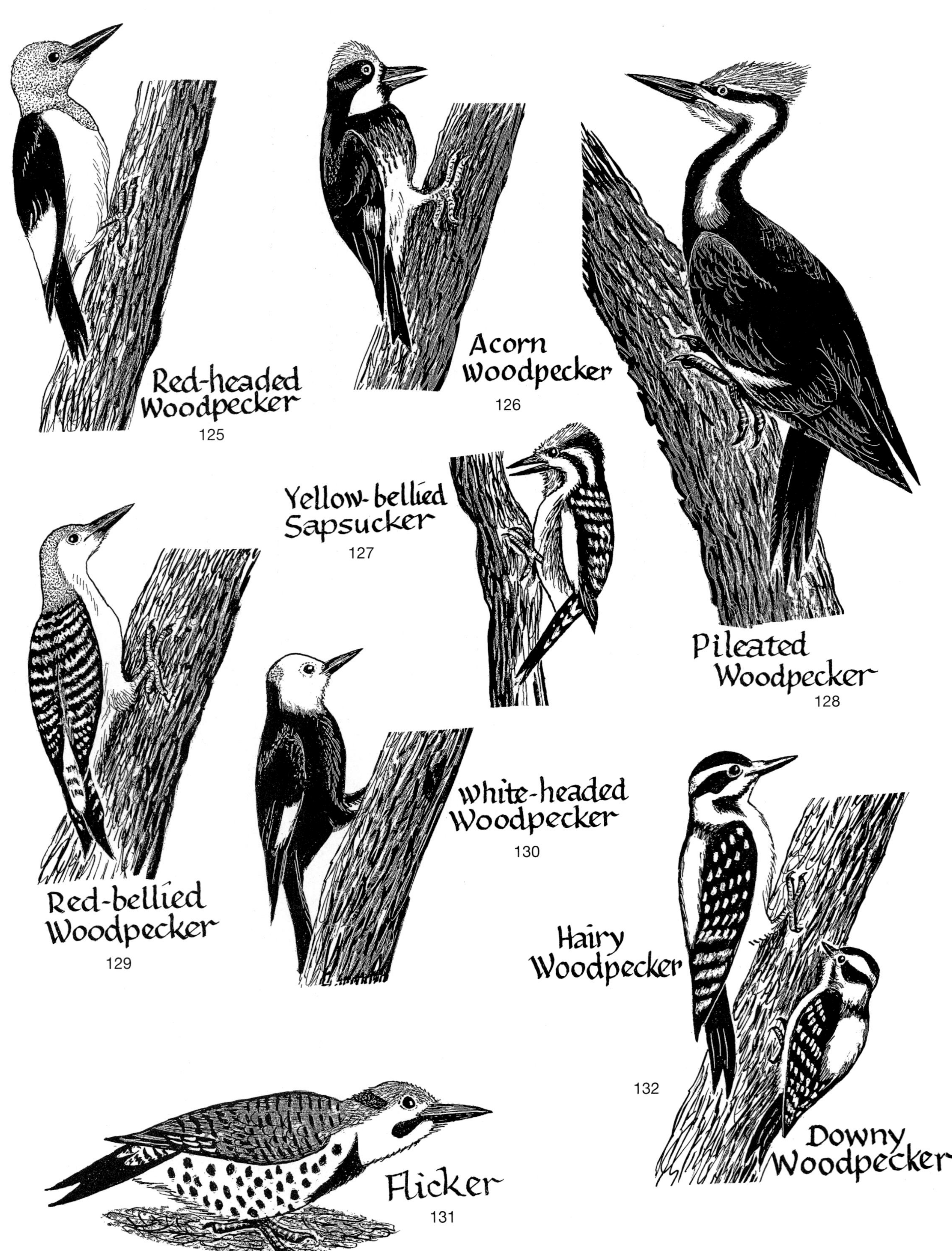
Red-headed
Woodpecker
125
Acorn
Woodpecker
126
Yellow-bellied
Sapsucker
127
Pileated
Woodpecker
128
Red-bellied
Woodpecker
129
White-headed
Woodpecker
130
Hairy
Woodpecker
132
Flicker
131
Downy
Woodpecker

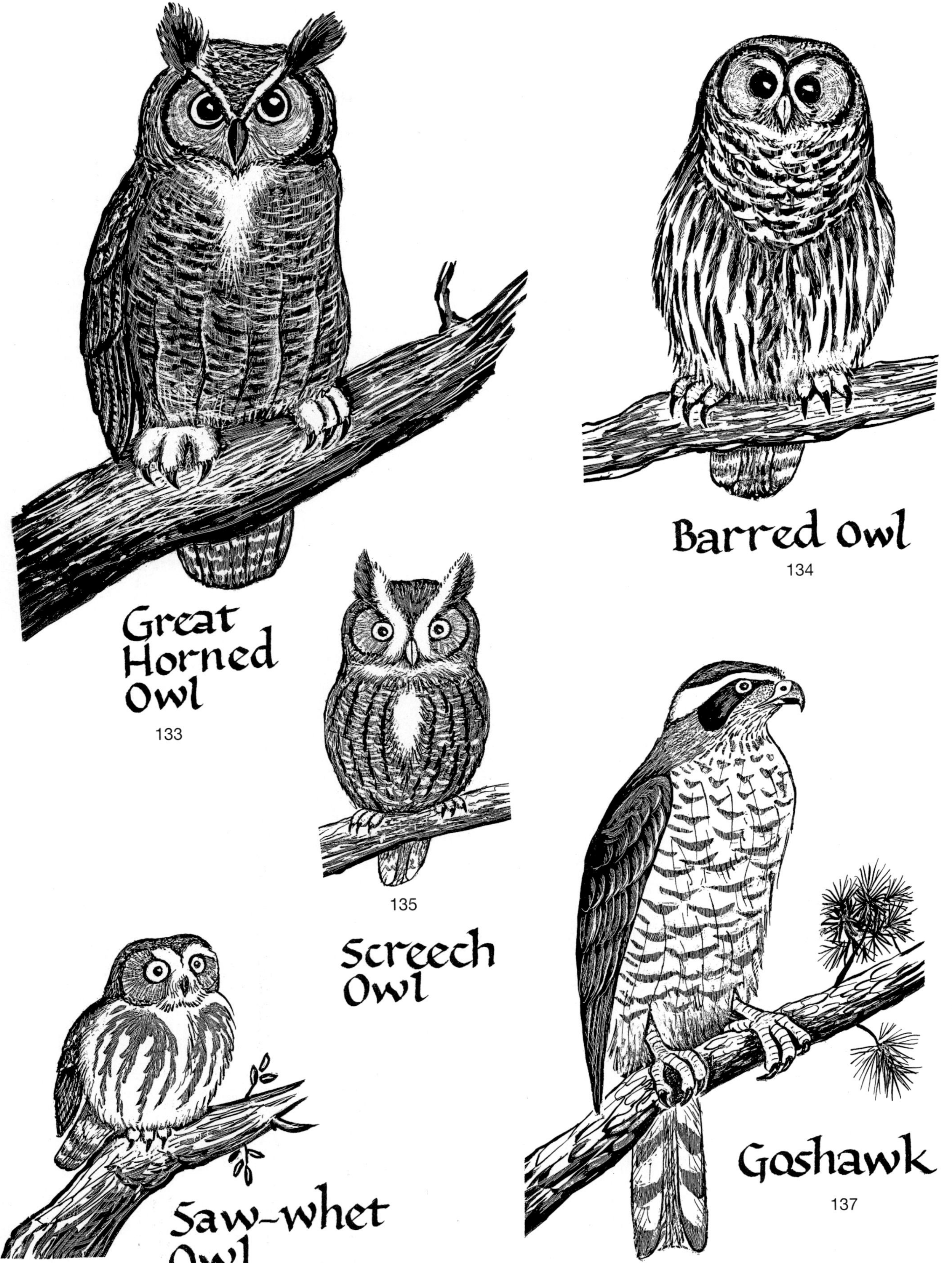

Great
Horned
Owl
133
Barred Owl
134
Screech
Owl
135
Saw-whet
Owl
136
Goshawk
137

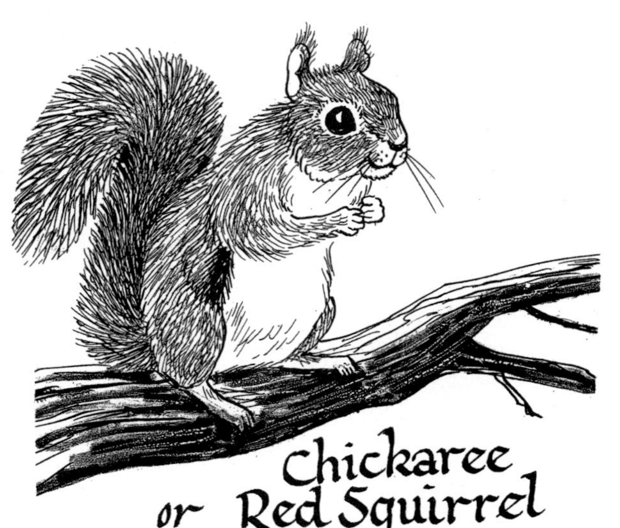

Chickaree
or Red Squirrel

138

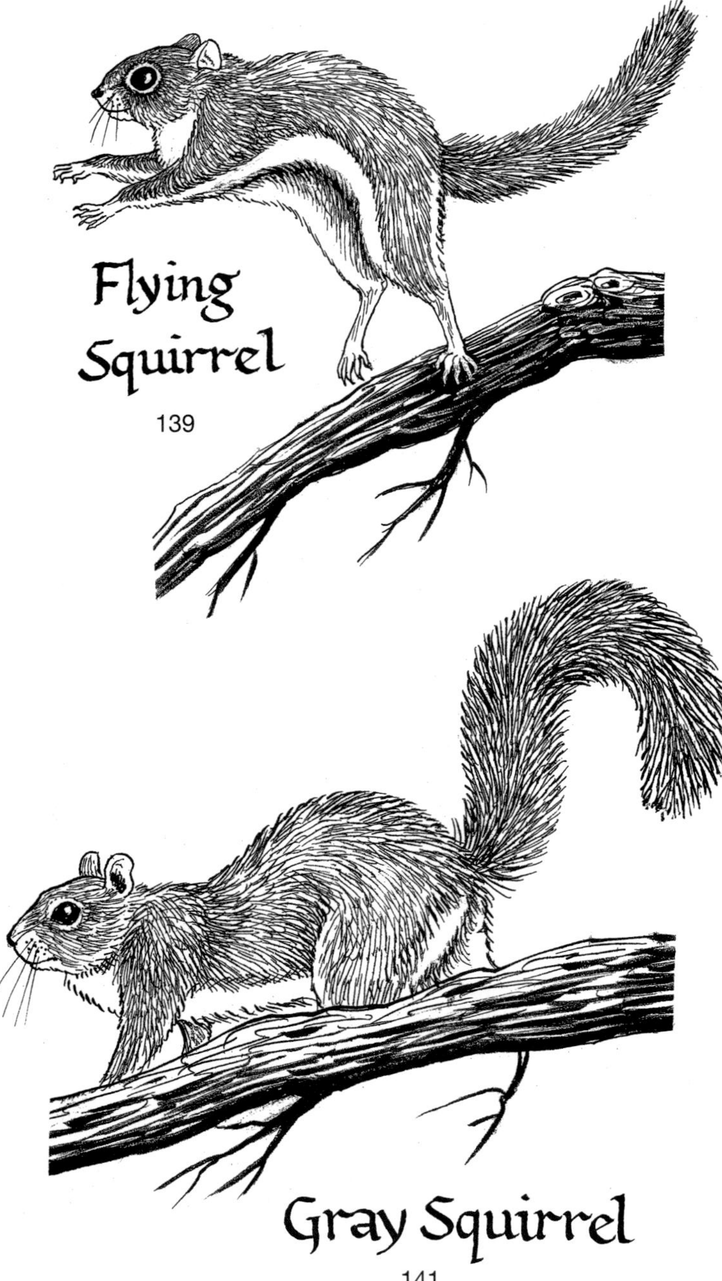

Flying
Squirrel

139

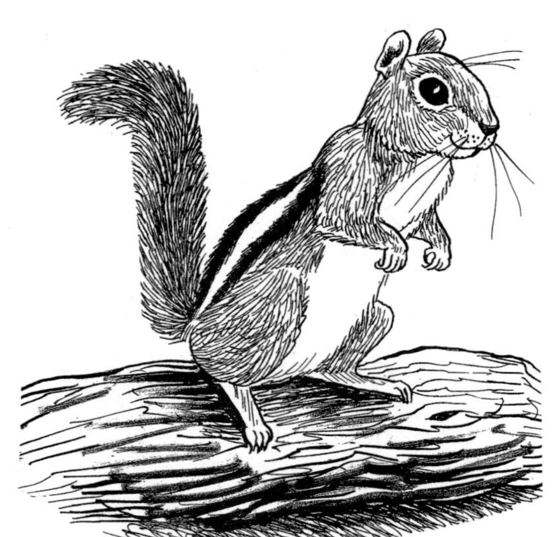

140 Golden-mantled
Ground Squirrel

Gray Squirrel

141

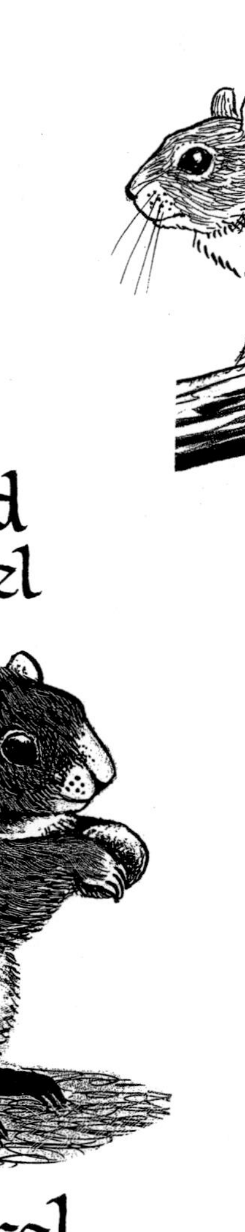

Fox Squirrel

142

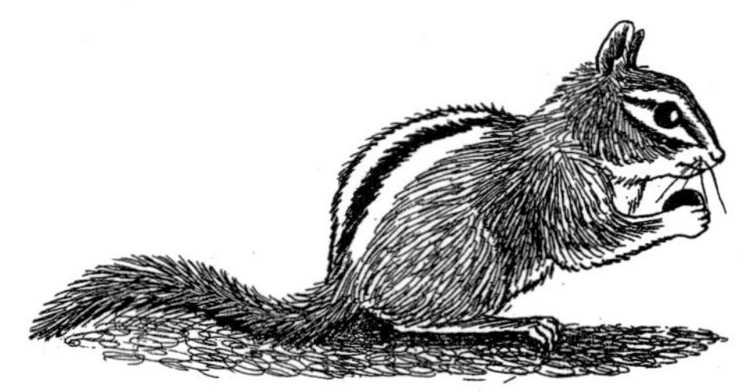

Chipmunk

143

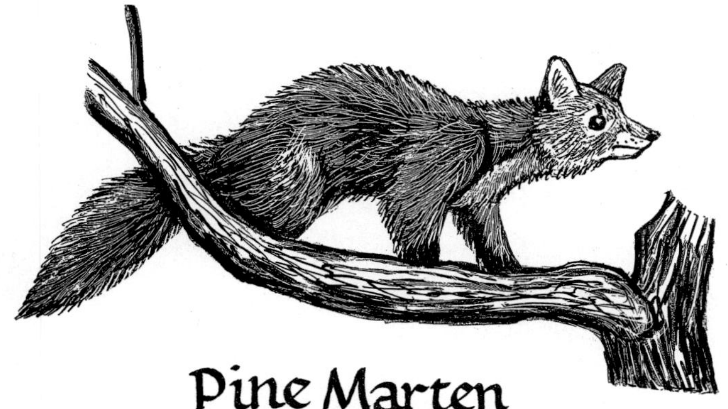

Pine Marten
or Sable

144

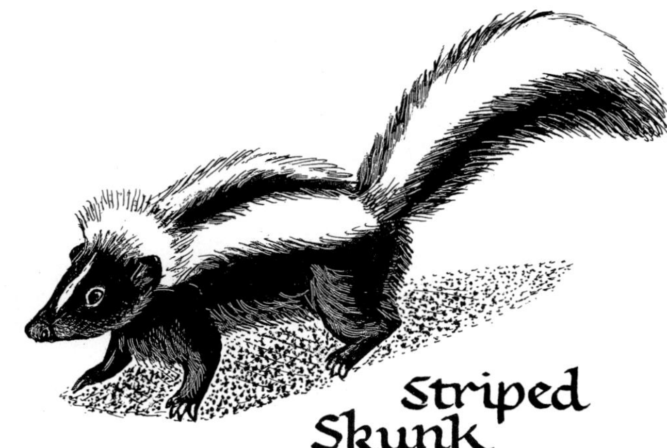

Striped
Skunk

145

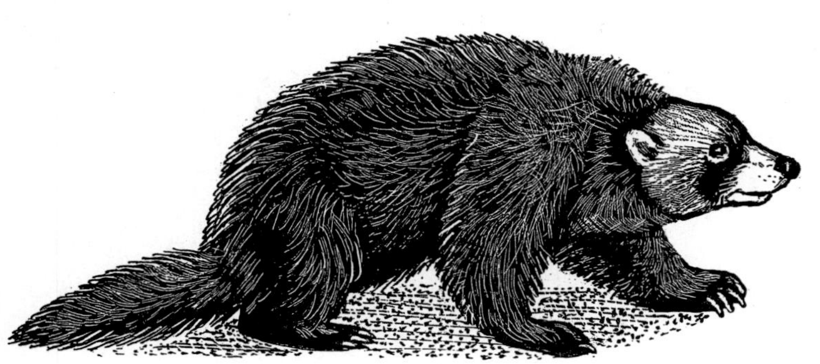

146 Wolverine

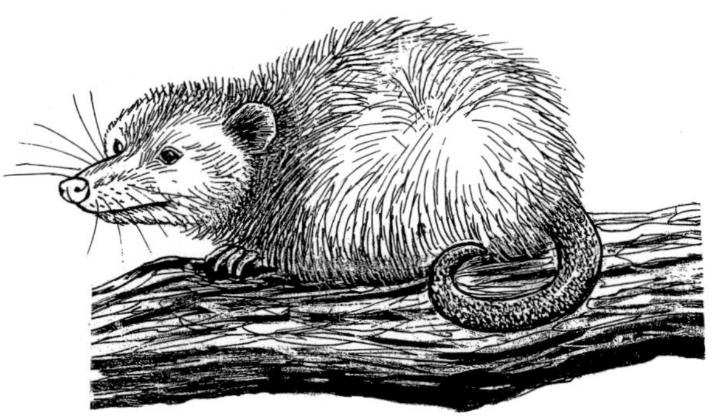

Opossum

147

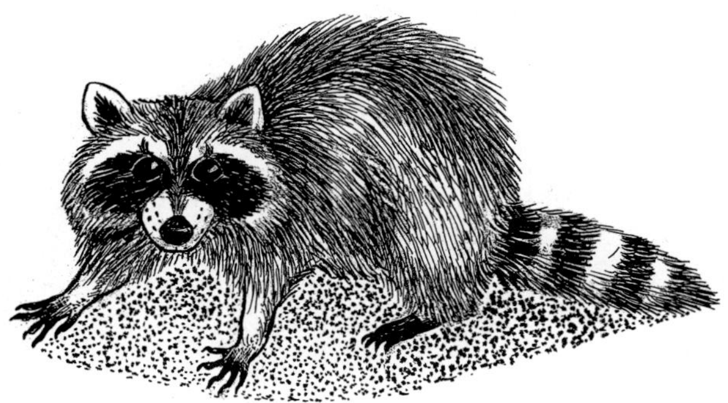

Raccoon

148

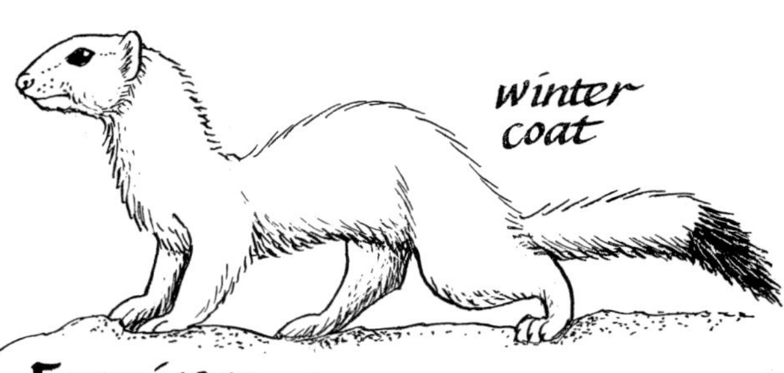

Ermine or
Long-tailed Weasel

149

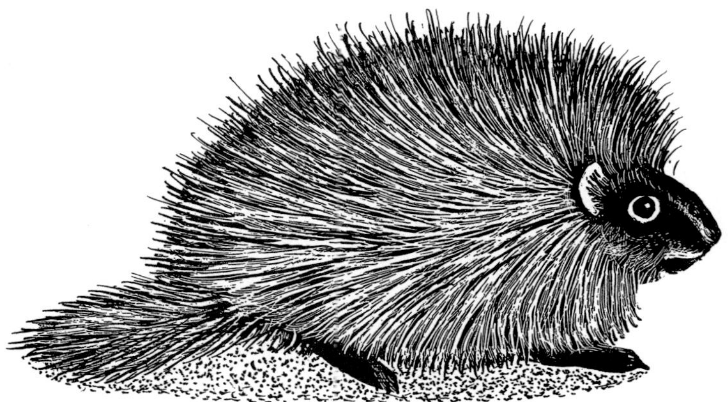

Porcupine
150

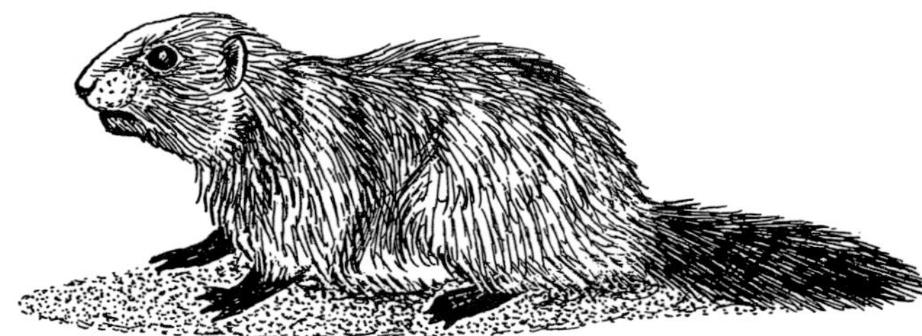

Groundhog
151

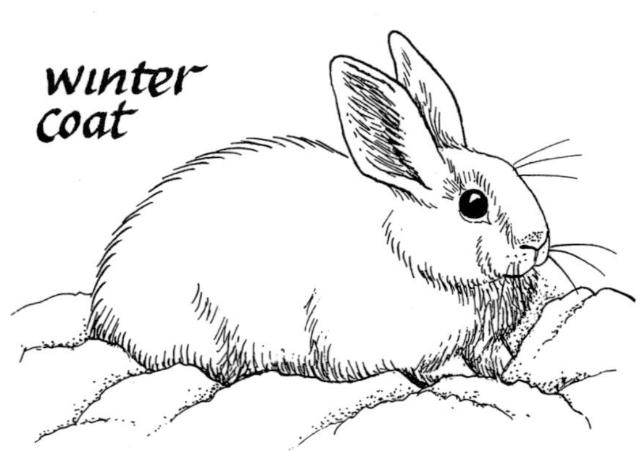

Snowshoe Hare
152

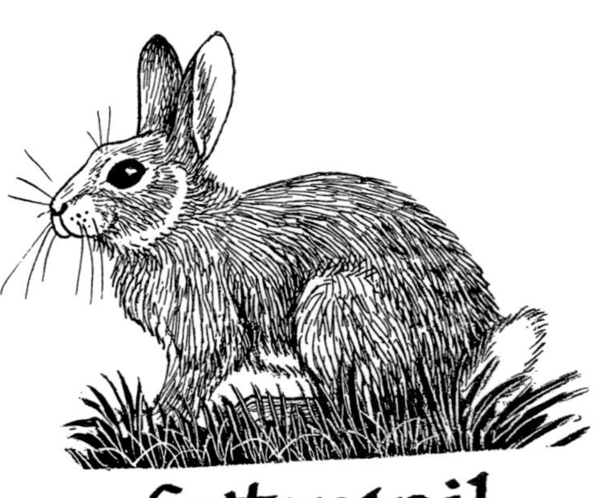

Cottontail Rabbit
153

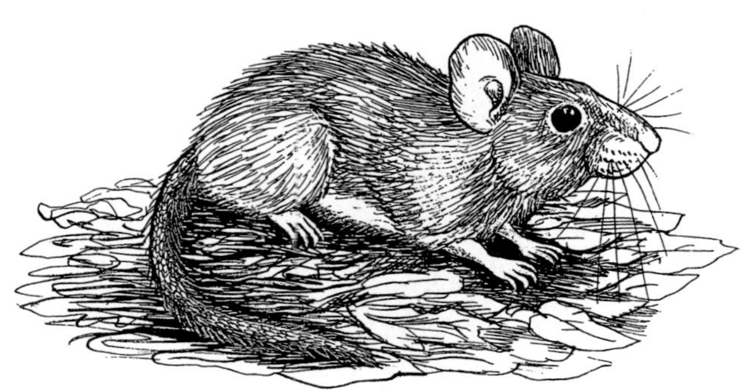

Woodrat
154

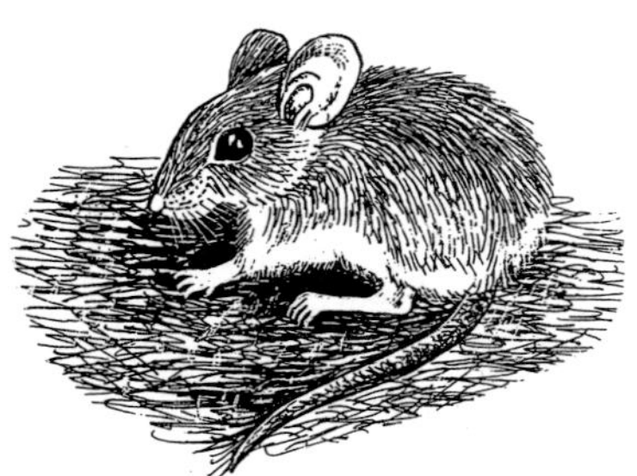

White-footed Mouse
155

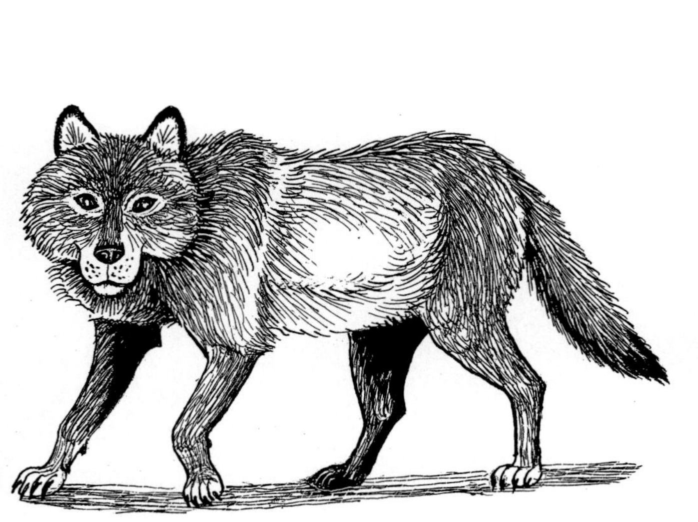

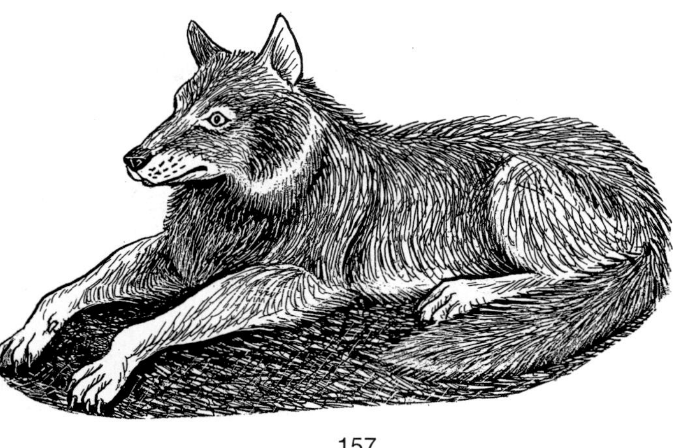

156

157

Gray Wolf

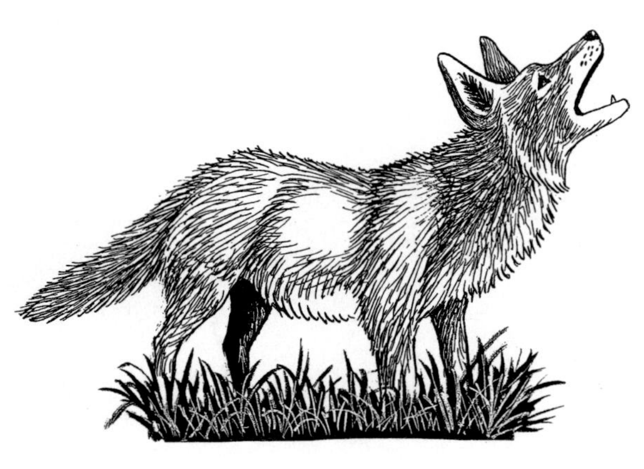

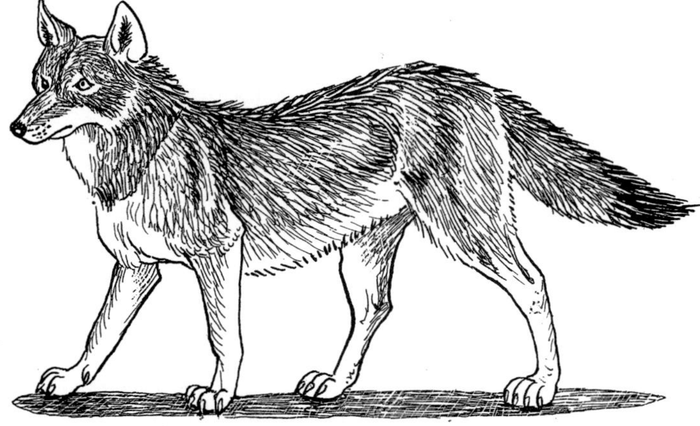

Coyote

158

Red Wolf

159

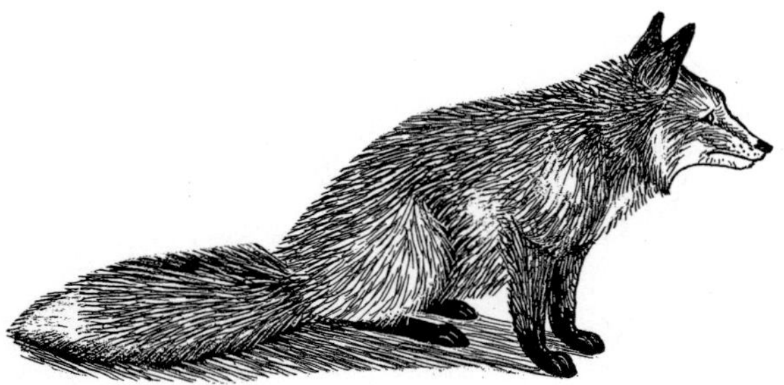

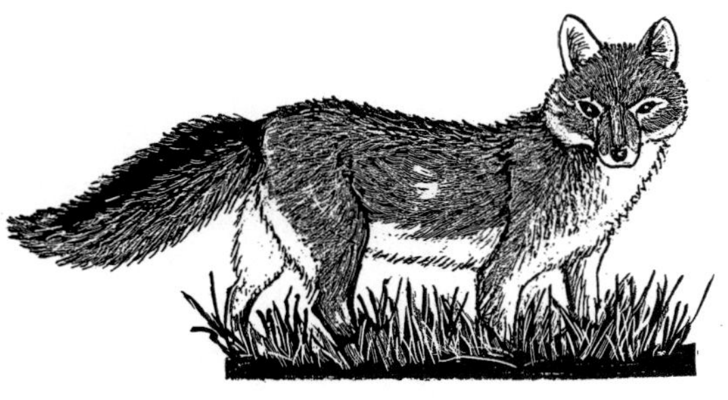

Red Fox

160

Gray Fox

161

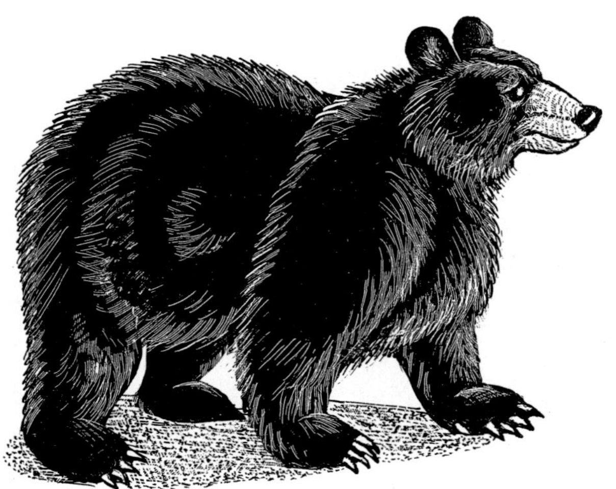

Black Bear

162

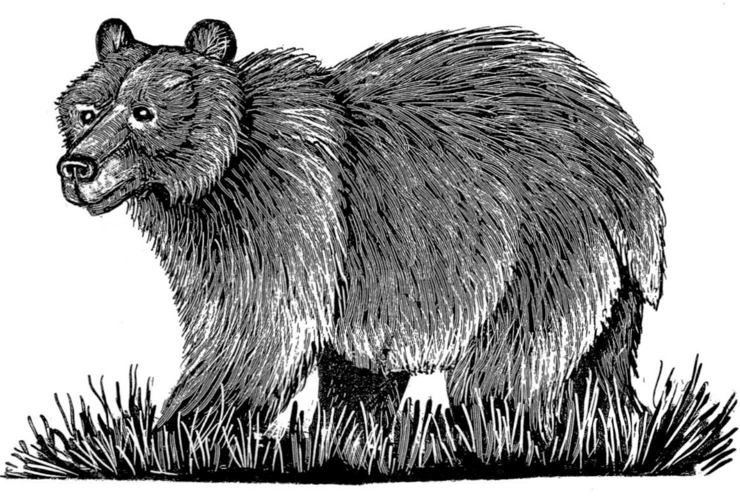

Grizzly Bear

163

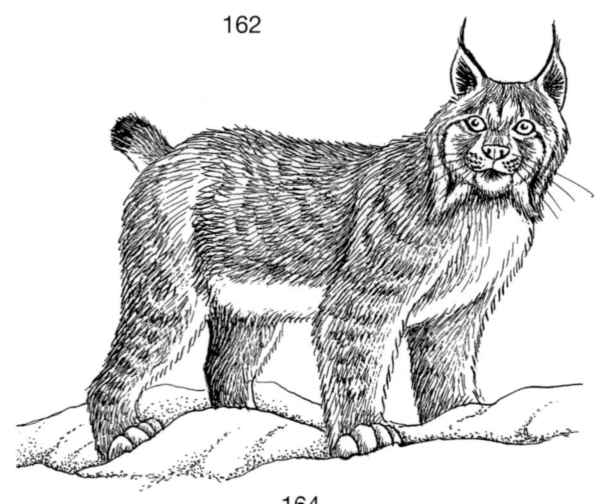

164

North American Lynx

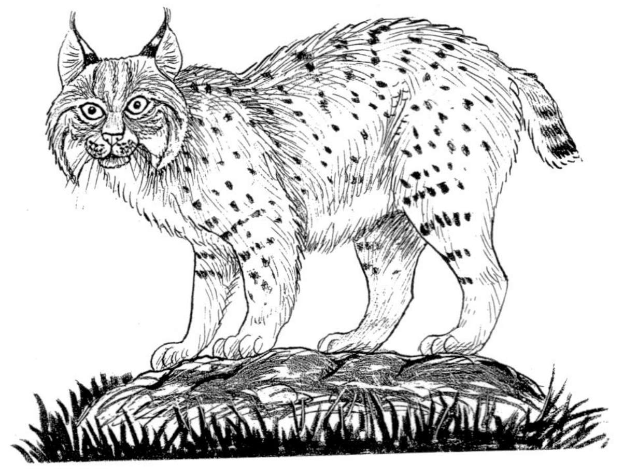

Bobcat

165

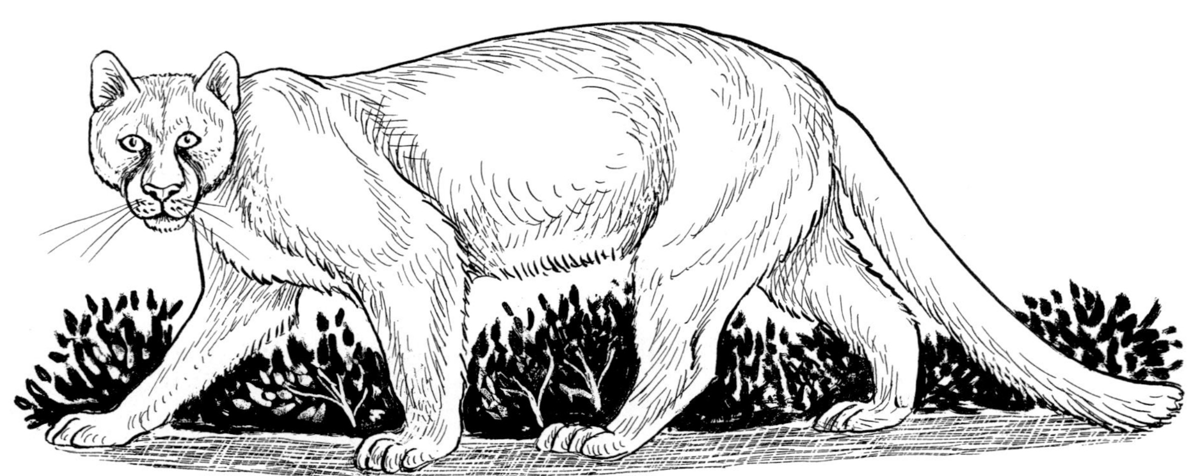

Cougar *or* Mountain Lion

166

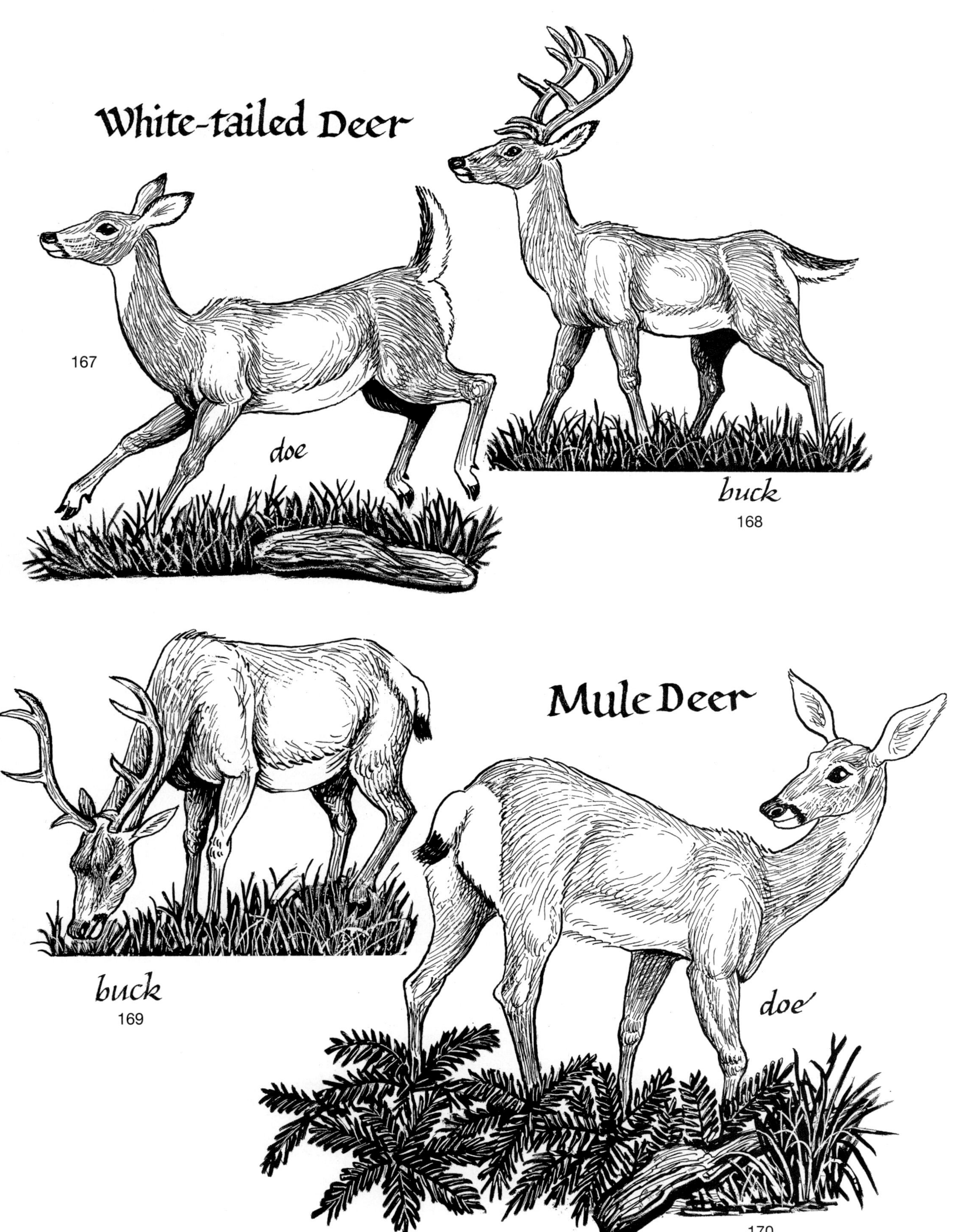

White-tailed Deer
doe
167
buck
168
buck
169
Mule Deer
doe
170

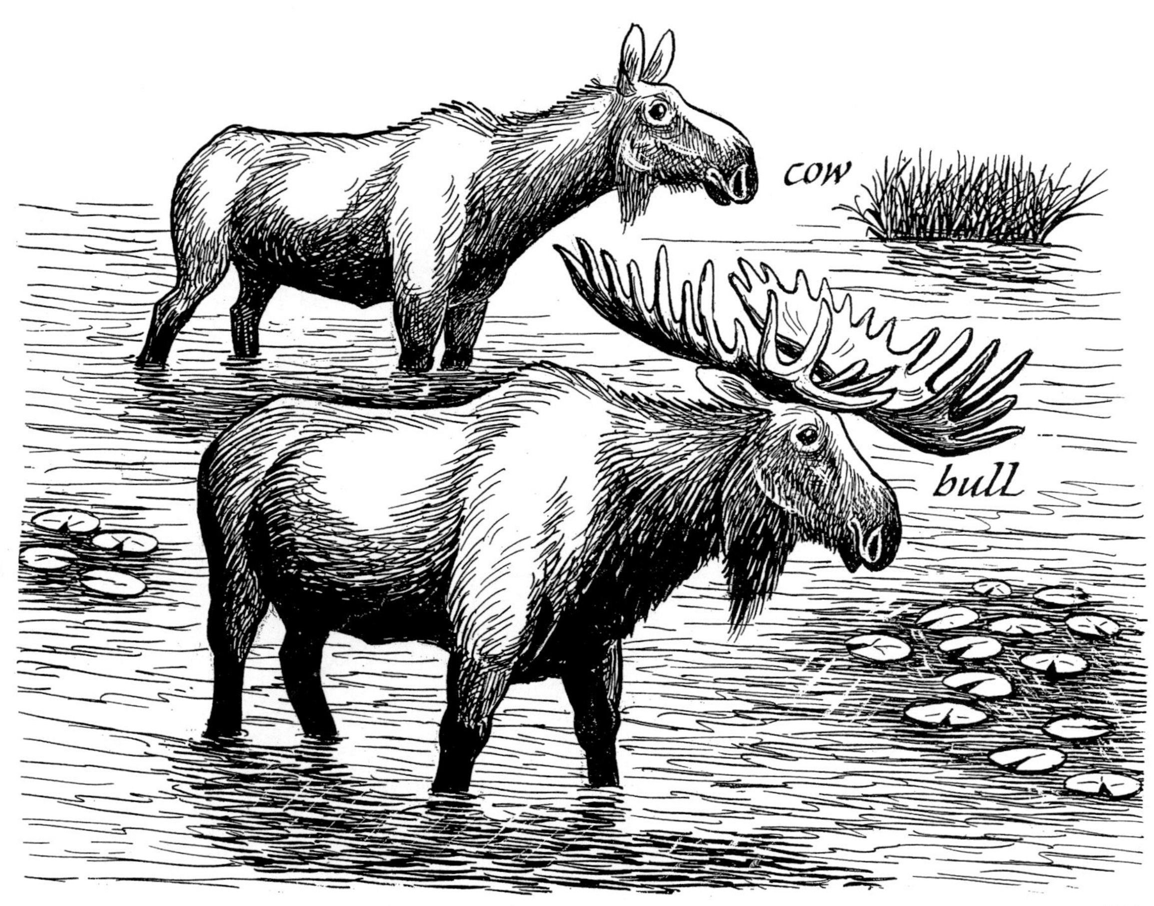

Moose

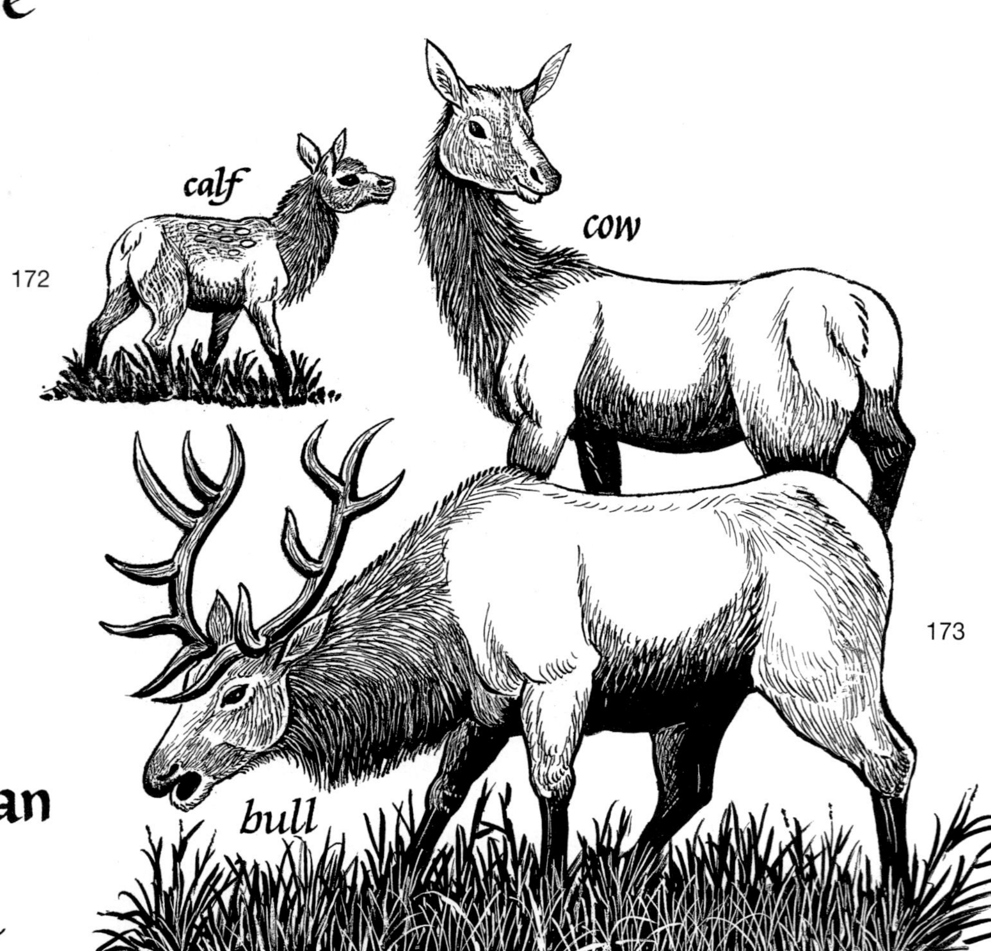

American Elk or Wapiti